FREE GRACE AND
DYING LOVE

FREE GRACE AND DYING LOVE

Morning Devotions
by Susannah Spurgeon

(previously published as
A Carillon of Bells)

— *WITH* —

THE LIFE OF SUSANNAH SPURGEON

CHARLES RAY

THE BANNER OF TRUTH TRUST

THE BANNER OF TRUTH TRUST
3 Murrayfield Road, Edinburgh EH12 6EL, UK
P O Box 621, Carlisle, PA 17013, USA

© The Banner of Truth Trust 2006
ISBN-10: 0 85151 918 0
ISBN-13: 978 0 85151 918 0

Typeset in 12/15 pt Adobe Caslon
at the Banner of Truth Trust

Printed in the U.S.A.
by Versa Press, Inc.,
East Peoria, IL

Contents

THE LIFE OF SUSANNAH SPURGEON

I

A Carillon of Bells

He that spared not his own Son, . . . how shall he not with him also freely give us all things? (Rom. 8:32).

❦

*D*EAR *L*ORD, faith's fingers are joyfully touching the keys of this carillon of sweet bells this morning, and making them ring jubilantly to the praise of your Name!

> *How shall he not!*
> *How shall he not!*
> *He that spared not!*
> *How shall he not!*

What a peal of absolute triumph it is! Not a note of doubt or uncertainty mars the heavenly music. Awake, my heart, and realize that it is *your faith* which is making such glorious melody! You can scarcely believe it for gladness?

Yet it is happily true, for the Lord himself has given the grace, and then accepts the tribute of gratitude and praise which that grace brings. Press the tuneful keys again, for faith holds festival today, and the joy of assurance is working wonders.

> *He that spared not!*
> *How shall he not!*

Hear how the repeated negatives gloriously affirm the fact of his readiness to bless! These silver bells have truly the power to drive away all evil things.

'He that spared not his own Son.' He gave his most precious treasure; *could* he withhold any lesser good from you? He has given you pounds; will he refuse you pence? No; while faith is thus quickened into lively exercise by the Spirit of God, the cadences of exulting praise *must* ring out, clear and loud, *'How shall he not with him also freely give us all things?'*

Think well, my heart, what 'all things' mean to you! If you have Christ, then *along with him*, and included in him, you possess *'all things'*. All spiritual blessings, rich and precious, are laid up for you in this divine storehouse, and God's choicest and most excellent gifts are here waiting for your faith to claim them. Rejoice, my soul, that Christ and 'the things of Christ' cannot be divided. Pardon, peace, sanctification, close communion with Jesus, and the indwelling of the Holy Spirit – are not all these gathered together 'with him' as a cluster of ripe grapes on a choice vine? Having him, you have all else. There is not a need or desire of your inner life which cannot be triumphantly met by faith's unwavering challenge, *'How shall he not?'* Nor is there a necessity of your temporal state which cannot equally claim the blessing of possessing 'all things' in Christ.

Lord, quicken my faith, give me to see how deep and wide, and full and free, is the unspeakable love which spared not your own Son, and therefore *can spare* every other gift, to me, your undeserving child! I thank you that it is not ''way over Jordan, Lord', that I must go to 'ring these charming bells'; but here, now, in the sanctuary of my heart, and all day long in the open cloisters of my daily life, I may make your glad music resound to your glory, and my own exceeding happiness –

> *How shall he not!*
> *How shall he not!*

2

Jesus Christ
Himself

*Our Lord Jesus Christ himself, and God, even our
Father, which hath loved us* (2 Thess. 2:16).

'Oᴜʀ Loʀᴅ Jᴇsᴜs Cʜʀɪsᴛ ʜɪᴍsᴇʟꜰ.' Oh, the divine
mystery of wondrous love and pity enwrapped in these
few words! 'The precious things of heaven', 'the chief
things of the ancient mountains', and 'the precious
things of the lasting hills', are surely all gathered
together here; and, with a deep and unutterable longing, my soul desires to search and find them.

That 'name which is above every name' is sung by
angels as their sweetest song; but the tender *earthly*
cadence which my heart hears in that emphatic word
– '*himself*' – intensifies its melody to *me*. Never before
did a personal pronoun bear such significance, or convey to heart so dear an assurance of perfect sympathy
and love. We say sometimes of favourite possessions
that they are our '*very own*'; and when we speak of you,
dear Master, as 'Jesus Christ *himself*', there is an added
fragrance in the 'ointment poured forth', a personal
realization of what you are to us in your divine man-
hood, which draws us 'with cords of a man, with bands
of love'. It brings you so close to me as my Saviour, it
seems to reveal you as the One who can be 'touched
with the feeling of our infirmities', and who sympa-
thizes in all our sorrows because you were 'found in
fashion as a man'. '*Jesus Christ* ʜɪᴍsᴇʟꜰ'. I say it over

and over again till my soul is filled with its sweetness, and my heart is satisfied with the peace of believing that the Blessed One is mine, and that he loves even me.

'And God, even our Father'. Lord, help me to realize all that this wonderful relationship means to me! As your child, I may claim all that you have promised to give; and if I am living and acting as your child – dwelling with you, loving you, and obeying you, I shall assuredly find that your Father-love is ready to grant every reasonable desire of my heart. Dear Lord, when I see, as I often do, some earthly fathers, whose love for their little ones is intense, forbearing, and unspeakably tender, how much greater yours must be! I feel ashamed that I do not better understand the love of your heart toward me, your child through faith in Christ Jesus. How much greater is that love? I cannot work out a sum, Lord; but I know it must be infinitely greater, closer, and dearer, because you are the infinite God, and your love is 'from everlasting'. Oh, that I may have the spirit of a child when I draw near to you!

What little one is afraid to run to a loving father, and ask for all it wants? Never a doubt rises in a child's mind as to the supply of all his needs, and the direction of all that concerns him. The child has positively no care for the present, no thought for tomorrow, no fears for the past. Father knows everything. Father can do everything. Father provides everything. In fact, *father loves*.

'*Which hath loved us.*' O my soul, can you for a moment imagine what it would be of joy, and rest, and peace, to live out day by day such a child-life in the love of the Father? He knows you altogether. He understands all your individual peculiarities, sees your weakness and sinfulness, your sore temptations, per-plexities, and daily shortcomings; but he loves you notwithstanding all, not for any merit or worthiness in you, but *because you are his child.* You have believed on his dear Son, whom he gave to die for your sins; you have accepted his complete salvation, you have received the Spirit of adoption, and now, with confi-dence and perfect trust, you can look up to him and say, 'Abba, Father'. And does not this suffice to make you absolutely 'without carefulness', like a little child?

O my Father, teach me to realize how deep is the love of your heart to me, since it led you to give your only-begotten Son – Jesus Christ himself – to redeem me, and bring me home to you, my God!

3

The Gift of God

If thou knewest the gift of God, and who it is that saith to thee, Give me to drink; thou wouldest have asked of him, and he would have given thee living water (John 4:10).

O WEARY MAN, footsore and sorrowful, sitting thus on the well, asking for a draught of water at the hands of a poor sinful woman – you are my Lord and my Redeemer; I believe in you, I love you, I worship you!

Nearly two thousand years have passed since you spoke the sweet words which are now comforting my heart, yet with what power and solace, and blessing, do they come to me at this moment!

'If thou knewest'. Lord, you have told me who you are, you have in mercy revealed yourself to me, I know you to be that blessed *'gift of God'* which alone can save and satisfy my soul. The depth and compass of heavenly love are manifested in you, and you have shown me, not my need only, but the sufficiency of your grace and power to meet it.

I am an empty sinner, you are a full Christ!

'Thou wouldest have asked'. This, too, O blessed One, you have taught me and enabled me to do; and my heart's constant cry, 'Lord, give me this living water', is familiar to your listening ears! It is *yourself* I want; Lord, 'My soul thirsteth after thee, as a thirsty land.'

Not your gifts, nor your grace nor even your glory, could satisfy the desire of a soul which you have made to long for *yourself*. You, the Giver of all other precious things, are yourself the choicest, the 'unspeakable' gift! Lord, into the thirst of my empty heart pour the full stream of your living love! Give me yourself, or I die!

And having asked, I believe you *do* give, for your own lips have said it, *'He would have given'*, and I whisper softly to myself the blessed words, *'Who loved ME, and gave himself for ME'*, realizing the sacred, overflowing joy of pardoned sin, and peace with God, filling and satisfying my soul.

So, dear Lord, my spirit, like a weary bird, folds her wings beside this sweet well-spring of comfort, creeps into this blessed 'cleft of the rock', *and is at rest.*

4

*His Great
Love*

Not that we loved God, but that he loved us
(1 John 4:10).

———

As the precious balm of Gilead, or the cassia and sweet calamus of the holy anointing oil, so came these blessed words into my dull and aching heart this morning. Dear Lord, I thank you for them; you have taken them from your own Book, and spoken them to me with your living, loving voice, and they have quickened me.

I had brought to you, with shame and sorrow, a hard and insensible heart; I could only groan out before you my utter lack of both faith and feeling. The very *desire* to love you seemed to lie fettered and powerless within me, only an occasional struggle revealing its bare existence. Then, Lord, while I knelt in your presence, with bowed head and troubled spirit – tears and sighs my only prayers – you whispered those sweet words in my ear and they brought light and liberty to my captive soul. Blessed be your dear Name for this glorious deliverance! It is not my poor, cold, half-hearted love that is to satisfy and comfort me; but your love, great, and full, and free, and eternal as yourself! Surely, I had known this before, Lord; but I had shut myself up in unbelief till, in your sweet mercy, you spoke the word that released me from my chains, opened my prison doors, and let me out into the sunshine of true peace in believing.

'Not that we loved God.' No, and that is the sad wonder and mystery of the unrenewed life, dearest master. *Not* to have loved you, is our greatest guilt and shame. It is even worse than this with us, for we were enemies, by wicked works, to him who claimed the most ardent and grateful love of our souls; we had put ourselves in an attitude of *defiance* against our best Friend; or if not openly defiant, we were totally forgetful of him to whom our heart's allegiance was justly due. *'NOT that we loved God.'* Ah, dearest Lord, you know how deeply, sadly true this was of me, and how I mourn over the years pent without love to you, and at a distance from you! O hard heart, O blind eyes, O poor dull sluggish soul, that could be unmindful of the strivings of God's Spirit, could deliberately neglect the pleadings of a Saviour's love, and see no beauty in One who is 'altogether lovely'!

'But that he loved us.' Here is a blessed contrast, here is the antidote for sin's sting, here is light after darkness, hope after despair, life after death! Lord, my soul flings itself on this glorious *fact*, this saving truth, as a drowning man seizes upon a life-belt thrown to him in the surging sea! If you do not love me and lift me, I must perish for ever. But there is no question of sinking when Jesus saves, no fear of losing life when he loves.

O my Lord, how I thank you for this precious word upon which you have caused me to hope! Now, all the day long, my heart shall sing over the safety and blessedness of being freely loved, instead of fretting about the sad lack of my poor love to you. *'Not that we loved God'* is darkness and bitterness, and death eternal; but *'that he loved us'* is light and pardon, peace and everlasting life.

5

The Kindness of God

My kindness shall not depart from thee (Isa. 54:10).

SOMETIMES we like to think of the consolation that awaits us in heaven, when our warfare is accomplished, and our iniquity is pardoned; but here, in this precious word, we have comfort and help for the daily life and strife of earth.

THE KINDNESS OF GOD! It is unutterable, illimitable, unchangeable! Every believer has experienced it; but the whole host of the redeemed, gathered from all lands, throughout all ages, could not tell the heights and depths and lengths and breadths of this 'great', 'everlasting', 'loving' kindness which dwells in the heart of God for his people.

'*My kindness.*' Dear Lord, the words are sweet to my soul as honey and the honeycomb. They carry in them an answer to all my misgivings, a response to all my pleas, a promise of power to overcome all my weakness. I say to you, sometimes, 'Lord, how is it that you can be so tender and indulgent to one so forgetful, so unworthy, so inexcusable as I am?' And your answer is – '*My kindness*' – 'I have loved you with an everlasting love.' 'But, Lord, I am a worse and greater sinner than I thought I was; every day reveals to me some hitherto undiscovered evil in my heart, which must be displeasing in your sight.' Again you say, '*My kindness*' – 'I have put away thy sin.' 'But, Lord, I have no power to do right, I cannot of myself even think a good thought, much less live that life of holiness which you command and require.' And again you give me that sweet reply, *'My kindness'* – 'My grace is sufficient for thee, for my strength is made perfect in weakness.' Oh! That I had a seraph's tongue to tell, or a pen dipped in the praises of heaven to write, what his lovingkindness and tender mercy have been to me!

'My kindness SHALL NOT DEPART from thee.' God's negatives and affirmatives are like great rocks jutting out from the insecure and shifting sands of all earthly experiences. When a troubled, bewildered soul is enabled by faith to cling fast to one of these, all fear vanishes, all anxiety is gone, nothing can move it from its confidence and peace. We have all suffered, more or less, from the ever-changing influences around us; perhaps we ourselves have added somewhat to the sorrow which is in the world by reason of inconstancy and changeableness. But never, for one moment, has our God withdrawn the love with which he loved us from all eternity, never has he forsaken or forgotten those who have put their trust in him. Bless his dear name, there is no such thing as *departing kindness* with him; 'no variableness, neither shadow of turning'. It is true, our sins and our ingratitude may so grieve and provoke him, that he may hide his face from us for a

while; but even then, his love yearns over us so much that, as Joseph Hart sweetly sings –

> *Shouldst thou a moment's absence mourn;*
> *Should some short darkness intervene;*
> *He'll give thee power, till light return,*
> *To trust him, with the cloud between!*

'My kindness shall not depart from thee.' O my loving Lord, let the support and comfort of this precious *'shall not'* sink deep into my soul this morning, and strengthen me to face every difficulty, and resist every evil, and bear any trial with the courage such an assurance gives! Or, make it a sweet resting-place and refuge for me, Lord, where I may be sheltered from all the disturbing changes of the world around me. Though friends may grow cold, and times may change, and circumstances may alter, and old age may creep on, and infirmities may gather themselves together, and flesh and heart may fail – yes, though my feet touch the cold waters of the river of death – this promise will stand firm and true, and your kindness shall not depart from me *for ever*, for it shall present me 'faultless before the presence of his glory with exceeding joy'.

6

*The Exceeding
Greatness of
God's Power*

What is the exceeding greatness of his power to us-ward who believe (Eph. 1:19).

———❦———

*C*OME, MY HEART, satisfy and delight yourself, this morning, with the thought of what your mighty God can do for you – the grace he is able to give you now – the glory he is reserving for you – the uplifting, upholding, strengthening, and preserving power which is all invested in his loving hands on your behalf. Here is a storehouse of riches on which your largest demands can make no perceptible diminishment, and all this is yours!

'Exceeding greatness.' Yes, Lord, more vast and wonderful than my poor finite mind can conceive. Your power bids the sun pour forth his radiant light and heat – your power holds the stars in space, and hangs the earth upon nothing – your power rules the universe with a word! Is it not exceeding great? All nature shows your handiwork, and your wondrous power is as much seen in the lowest forms of life and growth as in the higher developments of your creative hand. All the discoveries of science, all the revelations of its secrets which have of late so surprised and delighted us, are but glimpses of the infinite might and wisdom of the God whose 'love is as great as his power, and knows neither measure nor end'.

But, Lord, it is not on the majesty of your omnipotence as shown in your material world that I would meditate at this moment; it is the *'power to us-ward who believe'* that enchains my heart, and thrills my soul with joy. Help me to draw near to you, dear Lord, humbly and reverently, that I may 'see this great sight'; for though this is holy ground, and the bush burns with fire, there is no barrier as of old, to prevent a near approach to you, seeing that, now, we are made nigh by the blood of Christ'.

If I have true faith in the Lord Jesus Christ, then the exceeding greatness of the power of the Most High God, 'according to the working of his mighty power', is to me-ward, is on my side, or – I say it with deep reverence – *at my service,* always at hand to help, to guard, to defend, and to provide for me. My pen pauses as I ask myself, 'Do I believe this? Do any Christians really hold this faith? Is it possible that there can be among the feeble, doubting, self–engrossed, and half–hearted people that I see and hear of, any who possess the assurance that the power of the living God dwells in them, and that they 'can do all things through Christ which strengtheneth' them? If there be any such, why, oh! Why do they not walk worthy of the vocation wherewith they are called'?

Look to yourself, my soul. Is the exceeding greatness of your Lord's power manifest in you as it should be?

Blessed be his Name, you can say, 'He has redeemed me from death and hell, pardoned my sins through the shedding of his precious blood, and given me a promise of life eternal in his presence.' But what more? Those are the cardinal gifts of his grace, the cornerstones of his mercy and love. What do you possess of the *details* of his mighty working, the filling up, as it were, of the great plan of his will and design concerning you? What does 'the effectual working of his power' produce in your heart and life? Are you wholly consecrated to his service? Have you given yourself and all that you have into his loving hands? Are you filled with his Holy Spirit? Does he control every thought and word and deed? Are all the powers of your being and all the possessions of both soul and body subject and surrendered to his absolute sway?

Ah, Lord! Your poor child sorrowfully confesses to falling very far short of the high standard of Christian life to which your Word expects us to attain. In common with so many others, I seem to live at a 'poor dying rate' when I might have 'life more abundantly'. I know the possibilities of conformity to Christ are only to be measured by the exceeding riches of your grace, and the exceeding greatness of your power, and yet I sometimes seem content without a full participation in the glorious experience which your love offers. Lord, enlighten and quicken me, I beg you!

Put forth in me the mighty grace which will make my daily life a proof that you are working your own will in me, and giving me to know at least in some measure, 'what is the exceeding greatness of his power to us-ward who believe'.

7

The Mourners' Comforter

The Lord GOD will wipe away tears from off all faces
(Isa. 25:8).

Come, all you sorrowful, mourning souls and see what a fair pearl of promise your God has brought to light for you, out of the very depths of the sea of your affliction. Here is an assurance so inexpressibly tender, a fact so blessed and joyful, that you can hardly regret the weeping which is to enlist such divine sympathy and consolation.

Come, and we will together – for I also am a mourner – look into this precious word of our God; we will dwell upon its unspeakable love, we will think upon its gentle pity, till our tears catch its soft radiance, and glisten with the beauty of the 'rainbow round about the throne'.

I have sometimes wondered whether that glorious arch, encircling the very throne of God, can be typical of the transformation of earth's sorrows into heavenly joys – a lovely symbol of the shining of God's pardoning love upon the rain of tears from mortal eyes, for sin, and suffering, and death. There can be no rainbow without showers, you know, and certainly there can be no weeping in heaven; so, may it not be that the Lord has put this 'appearance of the bow that is in the cloud in the day of rain' in his high and holy place, as a token to us that all the tears we shed on earth are reflected up in heaven, and gleam there in fair colours, as the light of his love to us in Christ Jesus falls tenderly upon them? 'I have seen your tears', he says, 'they shall all be wiped away some day.'

How often are we constrained to cry, 'Mine eyes do fail with tears' for the *sin* which still rises up with terrible force in our heart, and how constantly have we to weep over the evil which is present with us! Such tears are silent but eloquent witnesses of our repentance towards God, and faith in the Lord Jesus Christ, and no jewels can be so attractive and precious in his sight as the tears of a sinner for his sin. Yet these tears shall all be wiped away some day.

The salt drops which steal down our cheeks through physical *suffering* – wrung from our eyes by mortal pain and weakness are all seen by our loving Lord; they are put into his bottle; his purpose concerning them shall be manifest when their mission is accomplished, and then the source from whence they sprang shall be for ever dried up. 'God shall wipe away all tears from their eyes.'

And with what inconceivable tenderness shall the bitter tears caused by *bereavement* be wiped away when we get home! Here, the deep waters of our sorrow seem to be assuaged for a little while, only to burst forth again with greater power to deluge our hearts with the memory of past anguish; but how completely will all traces of grief vanish there! When we see for ourselves the glory of that land to where our loved ones have passed before us, our wonder will be that we could have sorrowed at all at sparing them from life's woes to enter into the 'fulness of joy' at God's right hand.

'The Lord GOD will.' There is not the shadow of a doubt about this, poor sighing soul. Not only did our Father inspire his prophet Isaiah to speak so assuredly, but, twice repeated, he gave the same sweet message to the apostle John at Patmos: 'God *shall* wipe away all tears from their eyes.' As a fond mother hushes her child, as a tender husband solaces his wife, so weeping one, shall your God comfort you when he brings you home, and your consolation shall be so complete that you shall 'no more remember your sorrow'.

Yes, the world is full of weeping; even Paul spoke of 'serving the Lord with many tears'. Every heart knows its own bitterness, and every heart has bitterness to know. Sin must bring sorrow, tears are the inheritance of earth's children; but in the city to which we are going, 'God shall wipe away all tears from their eyes; and there shall be no more death, neither sorrow, nor crying, neither shall there be any more pain: for the former things are passed away.'

Blessed be your dear name, O Lord, for this 'strong consolation' – this 'good hope through grace'. Tears may, and must come; but if they gather in eyes that are constantly *looking up* to you and heaven, they will glisten with the brightness of the coming glory.

8

The Loveliness of God's Will

Thy will be done in earth, as it is in heaven (Matt. 6:10).

𝒲HEN MY SOUL IS TOSSED on the rough waves of the troubled sea of this life, if I can but cast out the anchor of hope into the depths of *God's blessed will*, it holds fast at once, and the winds and the waves are rebuked.

Dear Father, I thank you that you have made your will so dear and precious to me! Once, in the midst of darkness and unutterable sorrow, you enabled me to say, 'He hath done all things well'; and now, though the days are calmer, the fast-revolving years bring round the time of sad memories, and I look back, and say it still, 'He hath done all things well!'

'Thy will be done in earth, as it is in heaven.' My God, I bless you for the most welcome and soothing thought that, while the dear one you have taken from me is joyfully doing your will in heaven, I, by your tender grace, may be doing the same on earth. I cannot do it as *perfectly;* but I may do it patiently, humbly, and acceptably. Lord, make this my daily desire and delight! How near this hope brings me to my beloved! 'He is with Christ, and Christ is with me'; there is but the veil of flesh between us, and that may be rent asunder any day soon, and then we shall be 'together with him'.

'Thy will be done.' This resting in the will of God is one of the most comforting and blessed experiences of the Christian life. To say, 'Thy will be done' – not in a reluctant or compulsory way, as if we were shrinking from some inevitable pain, but with a sincere and glad conviction that our dear Father is really doing for us what is best and most loving, although it may not look so to our dull eyes – this is glorifying to him, and supremely consoling to us.

God's plans and purposes for me, and for you, dear reader, were all made and determined on from the beginning; and as they are worked out day by day in our lives, how wise should we be if, with joyful certainty, we accepted each unfolding of his will as a proof of his faithfulness and love! When once I, as a believer, can say from my heart, 'This is the will of God concerning me', it matters not what the 'this' is – whether it be a small domestic worry, or the severance of the dearest earthly ties – the fact that it is *his most blessed will*, takes all the fierce *sting* out of the trouble, and leaves it powerless to hurt or hinder the peace of my soul. There is all the difference between the murderous blows of an enemy, and the needful chastisement of a loving father's hand! The Lord may make us sore, but he will bind us up. He may wound, but his hands make whole. How often has the Lord to *break* a heart before he can enter into it, and fill it with his love; but how precious and fragrant is the balm which, from that very moment, flows out of that heart to others! Dear Father, how many of your children can truly say, 'Before I was afflicted, I went astray, but now have I kept thy word'!

'Thy will be done in earth, as it is in heaven.' Lord, can such a thing really be? The attainment seems so high, so heavenly, so impossible! Yet, if it were not within our reach, you would not have taught us to pray for it. Doing the will of God from the heart must be at least the reflection, the copy, of the perfect obedience of the saints in light. Oh, to be thus beginning the service of heaven, while yet on earth! Practising *here*, to be made perfect *there!* Learning the laws, and manners, and customs of the land where our eternal inheritance awaits us! Say, my soul, are you thus diligently preparing yourself for your citizenship in heaven?

9

Thy Way;
Not My Way

Make thy way straight before my face (Psa. 5:8).

—◦◦◦◦—

DEAR FATHER, THIS CRY is going up to you, this morning, from many a tried and perplexed soul, who is fearing to 'wander in the wilderness, where there is no way'. Will you graciously bend down your ear, and listen to their prayer, and grant the desired direction and guidance?

'Make thy way straight.' Dear Lord, it is not that your ways are ever crooked or deviating, but that my eyes are bent on seeing pleasant little bypaths, where the road is not so rough, or the walking so toilsome, as on the King's highway! *My* way looks so enticing, so easy, so agreeable to the flesh. *Your* way means self-denial, taking up the cross, and the relinquishment of much that my heart desires. Are not these very things the guideposts which show me the right road?

Now, dear Lord, hear my cry, *'Make Thy way straight before my face.'* Compel me, by the power of your love and your example, to go in the narrow road; 'hedge up my way with thorns', rather than that I should take a step out of your way which you have laid down for me.

What if, sometimes, there be mists and fogs so thick that I cannot see the path? It is enough that you hold my hand, and guide me in the darkness; for walking with you in the gloom is far sweeter and safer than walking alone in the sunlight!

Dear Lord, give me grace to trust you wholly, whatever may happen; yielding myself up to your leading, and leaning hard on you when 'fears shall be in the way'. Your way for me has been marked out from all eternity, and it leads direct to yourself and home. Help me to keep my eyes fixed on the joy set before me, and deliver me from the very faintest desire to turn aside, and linger in the flowery meadows which have so often lured the feet of poor pilgrims into danger and distress.

Father, you have said, 'My ways are not your ways, neither are my thoughts your thoughts.' Truth, dear Lord; but then you lift up my thoughts to yours, and exalt my ways until they reach the mountain-top of obedience to your blessed will. Work this miracle for me, this day, O Lord; use that sweet compulsion which will delight my heart while it directs my steps! *Make* me to run in the way of your commandments, and I shall run gladly, with the blessed certainty that I shall reach the goal at last! Have you not given me a monitor within, which strikes a gentle warning note when my feet turn but an instant, from the straight way?

But, best of all, dear Lord, come yourself with me along life's road, today and every day! Let the abiding of my soul in you be so real and constant, so true and tender, that I may always be aware of your sweet presence, and never take a single step apart from your supporting and delivering hand!

> *O come! for Thou dost know the way:*
> *And, if to Thee I cannot move,*
> *Remove me where I need not say,*
> *'O come, my Lord, my Love!'*

10

God's Beauty upon His People

Let the beauty of the LORD our God be upon us
(Psa. 90:17).

WHEN I READ these wonderful words, this morning, there came to me, quick as a lightning flash, the solemn question, *'Soul, is this beauty now resting on you, and on all your daily life?'* Alas! there was no reply by speech or voice; but a bowed head, and silent lips, and the inward sighing of a convicted yet penitent heart, gave the only possible answer.

Then I sat down before the Lord, wondering and ashamed, and the multitude of my thoughts within me took the following form and fashion: Father, you know that I covet earnestly the loveliness of sanctification and would gladly obey your command to be holy; and if longings after complete surrender to you would avail to secure this special grace, I should possess it. What is it that so constantly defeats my purpose, and foils my efforts, and prevents the fulfilment of my most devout desire?

Dear Master, if your will concerning me be my sanctification, why is that will not done more absolutely in me? Can it be that I am unconsciously cherishing something in my heart that hinders the work of your Holy Spirit, and so the blessing you have designed for me does not reach me, because the way is barred by a will not wholly yielded to yours? Or have I been satisfying myself with mere empty desires after conformity to Christ, indulging in poor feeble longings in which there was so much half-heartedness that the Spirit of God was grieved, and would not reveal his power?

O Lord, pity me, and pardon me! Awaken my soul to an earnest sense of the solemn responsibility involved in belonging to you, and bearing your name! Rouse in me, Lord, a joyful eagerness to become all that you wish me to be! Fill me with that mighty influence which works in us 'both to will and to do' of your good pleasure! Yes, chasten and afflict me, Lord, if nothing else will serve to make me a partaker of your holiness!

'Let the beauty of the Lord our God be upon us.' Dear Father, *I must have this blessing.* Help me to pray the marvellous prayer intelligently, remembering at what an awful cost you have secured to me an answer, and glorifying you for the matchless love which makes me –

> *With his spotless vesture on,*
> *Holy as the Holy One.*

What has God done! I can see, only too plainly, the ugliness and deformity which sin has worked in my nature, and the havoc it has made among all the creatures God had formed for himself. If it had not been for this deadly thing, we should have borne 'the image of God' even now. Does the lily plead for its whiteness, or the tree for its lovely foliage, or the sun for his splendour? No, they are as God made them; they have kept their first estate, and are still 'very good'; but man, sinful man, has fallen, and he who was made in the likeness of God is defaced and disfigured by the evil within.

Ah! dear Lord, when you give us a sight of our own evil heart, we are overwhelmed with horror, and should soon be driven to despair, if you did not at once turn our eyes to that wondrous hill of Calvary, where One 'altogether lovely' made the great atonement which brought us back to you! That precious blood, which cleanses us from all sin, restores to us the beauty which that sin has forfeited; its royal purple not only covers our disfigurement, but removes it, and bestows upon us the beauty which the Lord looks on with pleasure.

O my soul, do you not desire above all things that this 'beauty of holiness' may be your glorious dress? Then you must keep very close to the Master, shutting the door of your heart to every evil thing, and opening it wide to the incoming of his Holy Spirit, who, in revealing Christ to you, will make you *like him*.

An old fable tells how a piece of common clay became sweetly scented by close contact with a rose; the fable will be a happy fact in your experience if the Rose of Sharon blooms in your heart, and sheds its fragrance around your life. 'Thine eyes shall see the King in his beauty', yes, may God grant it; but the condition is thus expressed – 'Holiness, without which no man shall see the Lord'.

Everlasting praises be to the Well-beloved of our soul that his perfect righteousness covers us now, and that in the day when he shall bring us home to 'his Father's house', we shall be 'PRESENTED FAULTLESS BEFORE THE PRESENCE OF HIS GLORY WITH EXCEEDING JOY'!

II

Divine Anointing

I shall be anointed with fresh oil (Psa. 92:10).

⸻✦⸻

*L*ORD, IF YOU WILL yourself put this confident language into the lips of my heart this morning, and give me the power to believe in you, then this thing that I say shall take place – I have your own word for it (*Mark* 11:23).

'*I shall be anointed with fresh oil.*' How wonderfully do your mercy and my need meet together here! My soul's necessities make a happy pretext for the outpouring of your grace. When your love wakens me in the morning – how cheering is the thought that this anointing awaits my poor listless, sluggish, corroded soul! The 'renewing of the Holy Ghost', the 'quickening of the Spirit', the 'coming of the Comforter' – these are the precious ingredients, which give 'beauty for ashes, the oil of joy for mourning', and make the face to shine with heaven's reflected glory.

'*I shall be anointed with fresh oil.*' O my dear Lord, you alone know the deep and constant need I have of this 'anointing which teacheth all things'. Sometimes, my spiritual life seems to come to a deadlock, like a delicate piece of machinery which is clogged by rust and grime. Scarce a desire heavenward moves the lagging wheels, only a feeble heart-throb, now and again, proves the motive-power to be still lingering within. 'My soul cleaveth unto the dust', and my whole being is deadened, till I cry, 'Quicken Thou me, O Lord!'

Then, in a wonderful answer to my call, there comes the whispered word of power and deliverance, 'I will put my Spirit within you, and cause you to walk in my statutes', and the soul feels the blessed softening and life-giving working of the Holy Spirit, as she shakes herself from the dust, and utters once again the glad assurance, '*I shall be anointed with fresh oil.*'

And oh, how easily and smoothly all things go when the Spirit dwells in the heart, and *sheds abroad* the love of God within and around us! All the canker and rust disappear from our daily lives, and with eager diligence we set ourselves to do our Master's will.

Dear Lord, your Word declares, 'The anointing which ye have received of him, abideth in you.' Fulfil this promise to me, I beg you, that I may no more dishonour you by languid or half-hearted worship or work.

Anoint me for *service*, Lord, that, in all I do for you, either directly or indirectly, there may be manifested the power of the Holy Spirit, and the wholehearted earnestness which only he can supply!

Anoint me for *sacrifice*, so that contrary to my sinful nature, *self* may be overcome, and bound, and crucified, that Christ alone may reign in my mortal body!

Anoint me for *suffering*, if so it be your will, that I may praise you as I pass through the waters and the fires of affliction!

Anoint me for *intercession*, O my Father, that for others, as well as for myself, I may plead with you, and may prevail! This morning, Lord, pour your holy 'oil of joy' upon my head, and let the precious, fragrant unction of your grace drop down from hour to hour on the day's garments, till the skirts of night shall enfold both body and soul in the sweet spices of the sleep which you give to your beloved!

12

Opened Ears

Cause me to hear thy loving kindness in the morning;
for in thee do I trust (Psa. 143:8).

THE EARS OF MY SOUL are stopped fast, Lord, until you open them. I am deaf, and cannot hear the music of the mercies which are singing around me, like sweet choristers from heaven.

'*Cause me to hear.*' As you opened the eyes of Elisha's servant, to see your armies of defence and protection for your prophet, so unclose my ears that the tones of your still small voice may penetrate to my heart, and thrill it with exceeding joy; or, if I am too deafened by the roar and rush of earth's turmoil and distress, speak more loudly to me, Lord, '*Cause* me to hear', lest I should miss the unspeakable privilege of listening to you.

'*Thy loving-kindness.*' Lord, what unutterable depths of compassion are covered by those two words! Your 'kindness' would be an undeserved mercy; but your 'loving kindness' is a miracle of divine condescension and pity. You not only rescue, you embrace; You not only pardon, you espouse; and the robe of your righteousness, which is wrapped about your redeemed ones, is lined with the soft ermine of your *tender mercies*. And this for *me*, Lord, so vile, so unworthy, so often ungrateful and forgetful! What can I say to you for this?

'In the morning'. When all around are sleeping, Lord, waken my heart with your tender call, uplift my spirit into true fellowship with you. Early hours with my God will sanctify the whole day. In my quiet time with you, Father, so fill my soul with the sweet sounds of redeeming grace and pardoning love that, through all the succeeding hours, there may be melody within, and joy too deep and real to be disturbed or broken by any of earth's jarring discords.

'For in thee do I trust.' You know this is true, Lord. My soul rests in you; it lies down on the sure promises of your Word, and has sweet content. Yea, though this prayer, this desire of my heart to hear your voice, be not granted today, and you should be silent towards me for a while, it will be but your way of drawing me closer to you that, in tenderest whispers, you may tell me, 'I have loved thee with an everlasting love.'

13

Drooping Eyelids

Mine eyes fail with looking upward: O LORD, I am oppressed; undertake for me (Isa. 38:14).

—⊛—

*H*EZEKIAH had been sore sick when he wrote the Psalm, or ode, from which these words are taken. A long and painful illness had brought him to 'the gates of the grave'; and he here expresses, in pathetic language, some of the groans, and sighs, and cries, which were wrung from his heart during the time when he feared that he might be deprived of the residue of his years.

'Mine eyes fail with looking upward.' Upon first reading these words, my heart felt envious of the poor sick king's experience. What! To look up to God so constantly and continually that my eyes should be wearied with the *upward* glance? This surely would be a pleasant pain, a sweet sorrow, a most rare and blessed spiritual attainment. With me it is, alas! so different; my eyes mostly fail with looking *inward!* The fountain of sin within seems ever rising from the depths of my nature, and overflowing the banks of my life, and my gaze is too often riveted on the dark flood, instead of being lifted to him who has cast all my sins behind his back.

But I look again carefully at the text, and find that it should read thus, *'Mine eyes fail upward.'* The two words 'with looking' are interpolated, they are not in the original Hebrew. The meaning is, literally, 'Mine eye-lids droop, mine eyes are too weak to look upward.' Ah! now I can understand, and Hezekiah's words touch my very soul. It is as if he said, (what I have so often had to say,) 'I am utter weakness, Lord; a weight of sin, and sorrow, and sickness oppresses me, I am brought so low that I cannot even lift up my eyes to you; but come, sit by my bed, close to me, Lord, so that I need not *look up*, but can shut my weary eyes in the joyful knowledge that you are *looking down* in tenderest pity on me, and saying, "Fear not, for I am with thee."'

'Undertake for me.' Oh, the blessed restfulness of putting everything – physical, mental, and spiritual – into my Father's hands, and just leaving all there! When once faith can heartily make this transfer, all is well with the soul, and its peace is perfect. God does nothing by halves; if he undertakes our case, he will deliver us from all evil, he will blot out our transgressions for his own Name's sake, he will sanctify our affliction to his glory, he will turn our sorrow into joy.

14

The Details of Everyday Life

Thou knowest my downsitting and mine uprising, thou understandest my thought afar off (Psa. 139:2).

—◦◦◦—

THOU KNOWEST. Come my soul, here is a test as to your present spiritual condition! Will you apply it? Will you be weighed in this balance of the sanctuary, and see whether or not you are found wanting? Does your Lord's intimate knowledge of your every thought, and desire, and action, oppress and disconcert you, or are you willing and glad to live under such close inspection, and even to covet the glances of that eye which searches you through and through?

Nothing but 'full assurance of faith' in the precious blood shed for you on Calvary can give you *this* boldness. Happy are you, my soul, if you know that God 'looks through Jesu's wounds' on you, and through those wonderful ruby windows sees you so changed and beautiful that he can say, 'Thou art all fair, my love, there is no spot in thee.'

'My downsitting and mine uprising.' Lord, do you love me so much as to watch tenderly over me in such small matters? How the thought comforts me!

We do not care about the details of the everyday life of *strangers*: but when we love anyone very dearly, we take great interest in all that concerns them; and even so, my God, this searching, knowing, understanding, compassing, besetting, laying of your hand upon me, are all most precious tokens to me of your indescribable love.

How watchful and careful should this knowledge make me! *'My downsitting and mine uprising.'* My home life! My daily duties, both of work and of leisure! My going out and my coming in, my conduct and bearing under all circumstances! How these are all gathered into the compass of those five words! Lord, help me to walk worthy of you, unto all pleasing!

'Thou understandest my thought afar off.' What infinite knowledge! Well may the psalmist say, 'It is too wonderful for me; it is high, I cannot attain unto it'!

Before I think, God knows my thought! O my soul, are not your thoughts the source of most of your grievous perplexities and sorrows? They are often so unruly and rebellious, sometimes so unholy and profane, that all your efforts to bring them into captivity to the law of Christ are unavailing! Then, see where your help lies.

The God who can understand your thoughts *'afar off'* has the power to restrain them; no, more than that; before they reach you, while they are yet distant and unexpressed, he will purify and cleanse them, so that they shall enter your heart as angel whispers, and pass your lips only as words of love and blessing.

Dear Master, I make your servant David's prayer my very own and say, 'Search me, O God, and know my heart; try me, and know my thoughts; and see if there be any wicked way in me, and lead me in the way everlasting.'

15

The Troubled Heart

Let not your heart be troubled, neither let it be afraid
(John 14:27).

———❦———

*F*ROM WHOSE LIPS do these tender words fall 'like rain upon the mown grass'? Whose heart has such intimate knowledge of my need, and such profound sympathy with my weakness, as thus to meet both with the grace of his exceeding love?

It could be no other than 'Jesus Christ himself', my gracious Lord and Master, who thus speaks, and I shall do well to ponder each weighty sentence as I listen to his loving voice.

'Let not your heart be troubled.' Dear Lord, these words of yours, though so sweet, are imperative. They are a command, and should be instantly obeyed. Perhaps I have never before looked upon them in this light, never realized that, in carrying a troubled spirit about within me, I am acting in direct *disobedience* to your wishes!

'Open thou mine eyes, that I may behold wondrous things out of thy law.' Say the words over again to me, dear Lord! Speak 'as one having authority', and, with your gracious command, issue also the mighty power which will enable me to fulfil it. How often must I have grieved you by my want of trust in your tender love and care! How often must you have marvelled at my foolishness in attempting to bear burdens which might have been cast at your feet.

'*Let* not your heart be troubled.' Truly, I hear a grave note of rebuke and disappointment mingling with the music of these sweet words on my Lord's lips. It may indeed be so, dear Master, for after all that you have done and said, my heart should never be troubled, I ought not to *let* it be afraid.

And yet how soon does fear overtake the steps of joyful assurance, how quickly do I pass out of the light of your presence into the deep shadow cast by the mountain of my sin!

Lord, help me to reason with myself about this, for a few moments, or rather, say to me, 'Come now, and let us reason together', for then I know that your infinite love will conclusively silence my fears, and hush all the anxious restlessness of my soul.

Why should my heart be troubled? Is it on account of the overwhelming sense of sin and of unworthiness which sometimes threatens to crush all the spiritual energy out of my life? Then, I have but to turn again to 'the fountain of blood', and there see all my iniquities pardoned because laid upon the Sin-bearer, all my guilt forgiven because he suffered in my stead.

Can I keep a troubled heart when he died that I might have peace through believing? Can I have trusted *him* with my soul's salvation, and yet permit myself to doubt whether he has truly saved me?

Why should my heart be troubled? Is it the things which are seen and temporal, which are distressing me? The cares of this life, the struggle for daily bread, perhaps, or if not that, the thousand vexations and disappointments which are the lot of our poor humanity?

Come again to your dear Lord, my soul, and bring to his feet all that perplexes and grieves you; you will surely hear him say, '*Let* not your heart be troubled, neither let it be afraid; all your sorrows are known to me, and I am guiding and directing all that concerns you. Is it more difficult to trust my love in earthly sorrows than for eternal joys?'

Why should my heart be troubled or afraid? There is nothing on earth or in hell that can harm a soul who believes in Jesus. Every fear is put to flight by his perfect love.

Even the fear of *death* – so great a bondage in some lives – is lifted quite away when 'God giveth us the victory through our Lord Jesus Christ.'

Blessed Lord, help me to be obedient to your command, and to receive meekly your well-deserved rebuke, glorifying you from now on in my daily life by a restful faith, which nothing can disturb or dismay! 'The soul that on Jesus hath leaned for repose', ought never to know trouble or fear.

16

The Well in
the Wilderness

It shall not seem hard unto thee (Deut. 15:18).

D EAR LORD, I have this morning come to one of the secret springs of sweet waters; an ancient, hidden well in the wilderness which your love, as it were, kept covered up and concealed, till my great need moved you to open my eyes to discover it. How precious has your thought been to me, O Lord! How strengthening and refreshing are these 'cold waters to a thirsty soul', which you have thus made to break forth in a strange place! For I thought I was suffering a hard thing, Lord, in the dealings and discipline which you have seen necessary for me; and, though your grace kept me from openly murmuring and complaining, my inner self constantly cried out, 'This *is* hard, Lord, this is very hard.'

But now you say, 'No, my child, it must not even seem hard to you. Your trust in me should be so perfect, your faith in my love so strong, your obedience to my will so complete, that nothing should seem grievous which I appoint, no trial that I send should frighten or overwhelm you. Have I not always been to you "a very present help in trouble"? Lord, my heart says, 'Amen!' to your gracious words, and then trusts you to work all this loving obedience in me by your own mighty power.

'IT *shall not seem hard unto thee.*' The peculiar trial through which I may now be passing, is the very '*it*' which must not seem hard to me. God's bow is never drawn at random; he makes no mistakes either in telling the number of 'the stars', or in measuring out to me the griefs which shall teach me to glorify him. And, dear reader, if you would find comfort from the words which so comforted me, you must look upon your *present* trouble, *whatever it may be,* and say, 'Lord, this shall not seem hard to me, for I have received so much bounty and blessing from you, I have known so much of your pity and pardoning love, that I dare not mistrust you, or question for a moment the divine wisdom of your dealings with me.'

Ah! our eyes are so dimmed by earth's fogs and shadows that we cannot see clearly enough to distinguish good from evil and if left to ourselves might embrace a curse rather than a blessing. Poor blind mortals that we are, it is well for us that our Master should choose our trials for us even though to our imperfect vision he seems sometimes to have appointed a hard thing.

> *Ill that God blesses turns to good,*
> *While unblest good is ill,*
> *And all is right that seems most wrong,*
> *If it be his sweet will.*

Yes, it is in absolute and loving surrender to *the will of the Lord* that the secret of true rest and peace is found. This is the alchemy which turns earth's sorrows into heaven's blessings; here is the antidote to every sting, the cure-all of each care, the unfailing remedy for all anxious restlessness. Dear Lord, if I am your child, trusting, loving, obeying you, how *can* your will for me seem 'hard'? No, rather, I should joyfully meet and welcome it, well knowing that your love to me could only send a message of peace, however dark might be the envelope which enwrapped it.

This comfort cannot apply to troubles which we make for ourselves, and which we sometimes glorify into spiritual hardships, when they are really selfish sins; these are not God's will for us, but our own perverse way, and they bring nothing better than bitterness and tears. But a God-given burden or sorrow, carried out into the sunshine of his love, and laid at his blessed feet, immediately loses all its hardness and is transformed into a blessing, for which our soul praises the Lord with tender thanksgiving

'It shall not seem hard unto thee.' Ah! dear Master, it must grievously pain your loving heart when we, your own redeemed ones, think any of your dealings with us harsh or stern. You have loved us from everlasting, you did not spare your own Son when a ransom was required for our souls, you have led us, and fed us, and

cared for us all our life long; can we be so wicked and ungrateful as to deem anything 'hard' which your wisdom and love appoint?

'It shall not seem hard to thee.' Since this precious text rippled from the pages of God's Word, like 'a brook by the way', I have been drinking of its waters with great joy; when a trouble, great or small presses my soul, and causes my heart to faint within me, I take another draught from this sweet spring, and soon am ready to say 'It is no longer hard, Lord, for "I am filled with comfort, I am exceeding joyful in all our tribulation."'

17

Among the Furnaces

Every thing that may abide the fire, ye shall make it go through the fire, and it shall be clean (Num. 31:23).

⸻

*I*s THIS NOT YOUR WAY, even now, O Lord? The ancient statute has never been repealed, this 'ordinance of the law which the LORD commanded Moses' is still in force in a spiritual sense for his own Israel. His prey which he has taken from the mighty, his precious spoil which he has gathered from among all nations, must be cleansed and purified before it can be meet for his use; and so it comes to pass that all that may abide the fire, shall be made to go through it.

In this, surely, are comfortable thoughts for tried and afflicted souls. 'Beloved, think it not strange concerning the fiery trial which is to try you as though some strange thing happened unto you'; it was even so in the days of old and there is a necessity for the fulfilment of the commandment yet.

If we are God's gold, we must be subjected to constant purifying by fire. If he claims us as his silver, we shall be refined again and again, that our pollution maybe purged, and all that is true and precious may shine forth with fresh lustre to his glory. It is not the actual separation of the ore from its original dross that is here referred to, but the necessary cleansing of fashioned vessels and shapely treasures which have contracted any defilement, or suffered some dishonour. Alas! our hearts tell us what abundant need there is that 'the fire shall try every man's work of what sort it is'.

But now, dear Lord, help me to apply this your law to my own most valued possessions. Let me see what I have that will *abide the fire*. Will my 'good hope through grace' stand the test of such an ordeal? Will my 'joy and peace in believing' crumble into nothingness under the fierce heat of tribulation? Can the 'strong consolation' which God gives me disappear as a vapour when the flame of affliction touches it? Or, if I should lose my best and dearest treasures, can the hot furnace of bereavement burn up all my strength and comfort? GOD FORBID!

The true work of grace in a human heart *can* abide the fire of any trial to which the Lord may be pleased to expose it. We *can* sing of his love when the heat is most vehement, and glorify him by proving that promise true, 'When thou walkest through the fire, thou shalt not be burned, neither shall the flame kindle upon thee.' This is why the command is so frequently heard, thrilling through heart and life, *'Ye shall make it go through the fire.'*

Because our faith is precious, and our love golden, and our hope 'maketh not ashamed', they must be ever subject to the Refiner's fire. Does the flesh sometimes shrink from such a testing as this? Yes, doubtless it does; 'the spirit indeed is willing, but the flesh is weak'; yet need we not fear; the purpose of our great Refiner is to discipline, not to destroy us. He makes the sighs of the furnace to strike the key-notes of the new and everlasting song; and the coming forth of his 'tried gold' will be found 'unto praise, and honour and glory at his appearing'.

Dear Father, what a blessed reason this gives for glorying in tribulations also, for in this way we are being made perfect to do your work and will. What though the fire be hot, and the process a painful one, can we not see your eyes watching tenderly, and hear your loving voice saying, 'Fear not, for I am with thee', and does not your presence give 'fullness of joy' *anywhere*?

To *abide* the fire, is sure proof that we shall pass through it, and emerge at last in your likeness. You do not melt, and try, and prove that which is spurious and valueless; but, having seen the glint of the gold which is yours, even through the defilement which defaces us, you patiently wait, and 'perfect that which concerneth us'.

'It shall be clean.' O glorious promise! Not a moment longer than the furnace is needed shall we be exposed to its heat; but only when all that is vile is consumed, shall we come forth white and glistering. Dear Lord, we cannot love the fire, but we do praise

you for the fire's work upon us. By your grace, we would rather feel the hot breath of the purifying flame as it destroys our rust and rubbish, than disgrace our Lord and Master by living tarnished and corroded lives.

18

Testing Times, the Proof of Love

Fear not: for God is come to prove you (Exod. 20:20).

—◦◦◦◦—

I T WAS NOT from amidst the thunderings and darkness, the fire and smoke of Mount Sinai, that these words reached my heart this morning. They were whispered by a 'still small voice' in the quiet of my own room, and they brought courage and comfort in a time of painful need and depression.

'Fear not' – this was the tender message; and the reason for confidence was given – *for God is come to prove you*. The happy fact of his presence changed the appearance of all the things that seemed against me. The trial was not taken away, but my eyes were opened to see that, if it came from the hand of my God, there must be a blessing in it. My soul pondered the sweet assurance, and found in it the calm of heaven, after the storms and strifes of earth.

Whatever may be the grievous circumstances in which I am placed, or the injustice of others from which I am suffering, if my God says, 'Fear not', I ought surely to be brave and strong. If we can only get firmly fixed in our hearts the truth that the Lord's hand is in *everything* that happens to us, we have found a balm for all our woes, a remedy for all our ills. When friends fail us and grow cold, when enemies triumph and grow confident, when the smooth pathway upon which we have been travelling suddenly becomes rough, stony, and steep – we are too apt to look askance at the visible *second causes*, and to forget that our God has foreseen every trial, permitted every annoyance, and authorized each item of discipline, with this set purpose: 'The LORD your God proveth you, to know whether ye love the LORD your God with all your heart and with all your soul' (*Deut.* 13:3). O heart of mine, what is your response to this demand? Do you not love him enough to endure any test to prove it?

I remember once reading words to this effect – that, the moment we come into any trial or difficulty, our first thought should be, not how soon can we escape from it, or how may we lessen the pain we shall suffer from it, but how we can best glorify God in it, and most quickly learn the lesson which he desires to teach us by it. Had we grace and faith enough to do this, our trials and troubles would be but as so many steps by which we should climb to the mountain top of continual fellowship and peace with God. The soul that has learned the blessed secret of seeing God's hand in all that concerns it, cannot be a prey to *fear*; it looks beyond all second causes, straight into the heart and will of God, and rests content, because *he rules.*

'*God is come to prove you.*' My soul, think how great must be his love to you, that he should stoop to search for your heart's obedience and devotion! Think of the infinite God, your Redeemer, longing, desiring, yearning to be assured of your supreme affection! As he himself puts it by his servant Moses, 'Thou shalt remember all the way which the Lord thy God led thee, to humble thee, and to prove thee, to know what was in thy heart, whether thou wouldest keep his commandments or no.'

What pains he has taken with you! How tenderly he has borne with you! Every trial has been a test, every pain has had a purpose. And can it be that thou art still keeping back from him the full surrender of heart and life which his divine love demands? Still lingering and wavering on the borderland of half-heartedness, instead of gladly leaving all to follow him? No, Lord, it shall be so no longer! Help me to give you, at this moment instantly and eagerly, the proof of my love which you seek, in the submission of my heart to all your will, and the entire consecration of body, soul, and spirit to your service!

Then, every yoke will be made easy, and every burden will become light, for I shall carry them under the firm conviction that my gracious Lord has laid them on me, and is but testing the strength of the love and grace which he himself has given.

19

Briers and Myrtles

*Instead of the thorn shall come up the fir tree, and instead
of the brier shall come up the myrtle tree: and
it shall be to the LORD for a name* (Isa. 55:13).

◦⟨⊙⟩◦

*M*Y BLESSED LORD, how tender and pitiful are you to
me! What a delight it is to tell of your mercy and grace
to one so unworthy! Yet it is no singular story, for this
is your sweet way and will, dear Lord, towards all who
put their trust in you. When depression and sadness
come to me, by reason of the sin within, or the
discouragements without; when the thorns and briers
of daily cares and vexations prick and tear the weary
pilgrim's feet and hands; then you turn my footsteps to
where the pines and myrtles of your loving mercies
grow, and in their shelter and fragrance my troubled
spirit finds rest.

No, more than this, dear Lord, your power is so great
that you sometimes transform the very things that
hurt and grieved me into means of grace and blessing
to my heart and life. Disappointments in my work,
obstacles to its performance, the estrangement of
friends, conscious incompetence and weakness, and
often an overpowering sense of deepening responsibility – these experiences are all like thorns and briers,
which irritate and worry by their persistent and close
contact; yet all these vanish when you, my gracious

God, give the word, and I wonder as I find myself walking peacefully among the fir trees, where the pine needles lie thick upon the ground, spreading the softest of carpets under my tired feet; and where the myrtle's snowy blossoms and glossy leaves promise perfume and sweetness even to those who bruise them. Your ways, O Lord, are past finding out, but they are very gracious and tender; and this turning of seeming evil into good, of making your children's trials grow into triumphs, and their pains into pleasures, is a wonderful proof both of your pity and your power.

'It shall be to the LORD for a name.' My Father, can this be really so? Does your great Name receive added glory when you thus manifest your sovereignty on *my* behalf? When I come to the next sharp thorn hedge in my path, will it *honour* you if, instead of trying to force my way *through* it, and getting wounded for my pains – or attempting to avoid it by some roundabout course, and plunging deeper into the thicket, I should just calmly sit down before it, and pray, and wait for you to wither it up, or turn it into a myrtle grove? Yes, I believe it will, and I seek faith and grace from you to do constantly this otherwise impossible thing. Past mercies and deliverances should strengthen me to expect yet greater displays of your marvellous love.

Dear Lord, when troubles come, I should like to learn to look upon them as ways and means of glorifying you, to accept them as tests and trials of my faith, and to meet them with a brave heart, expecting the salvation of God!

If my path were always smooth and pleasant, with never a thorn or brier to vex and trouble me, there would be no opportunity for the glorious exercise of your love and mercy in deliverance from them.

Courage, my soul! Your God will give you grace to say as did his servant Paul, 'Most gladly *therefore* will I rather glory in my infirmities, *that the power of Christ may rest upon me.*'

20

A Cure for Discontent

Let my mouth be filled with thy praise and with thy honour all the day (Psa. 71:8).

---

*L*ORD, may this cry of my heart reach your attentive ear this morning! Lips, and tongue, and mouth are all empty at this calm, quiet hour, and I come to entreat you to cleanse and consecrate them to yourself and your service, so that 'all the day long' they may be filled with the sweetness of your love, and out of this blessed fullness may 'shew forth thy salvation'.

Far too often, O my Master, is my mouth filled with the bitterness of earth's impure fountains; but now, my chief desire is that only the bright streams of thankful love and praise to you should flow from it. How seldom does the tender grace of the early morning devotion *last* throughout the busy hours of the day! It is gone as the dew on the grass when the sun looks upon it, or as the fleecy cloud when the west wind blows it away. Why is it, dear Lord, that earth and earthly things have such power to draw away my thoughts and heart from the unseen but eternal realities which are so near and precious to me when I am alone with you? Will you not teach me the happy secret of abiding 'under the shadow of the Almighty'?

'*My mouth.*' This is a distinctly personal matter, about which I should be seriously concerned. 'All thy works shall praise thee, O LORD; and thy saints shall bless thee'; but if every creature and all creation were silent, this tongue of mine ought to speak of your loving-kindness and your tender mercy, for 'He hath put a new song in my mouth, even praise unto our God.'

'Filled with thy praise.' Abounding in thanksgiving! Brimming over with grateful love! So full of joy and rejoicing in God that, 'my tongue also shall talk of thy righteousness all the day long.' This is how it should be; but, alas! Lord, I have not glorified you like this. My heart has more often been troubled than glad, petitions have more frequently filled my mouth than praise, sharp and hasty words have escaped the lips which should 'drop as the honeycomb', and the glory due to your name has been less thought of than the passing needs of my sinful and selfish heart. O Lord Jesus Christ, how much you have to pardon and to pity! How very far I am yet from being conformed to your likeness!

A surly servant is no credit to his master, a thankless guest is no joy in a house, and a miserable Christian is an anomaly in God's universe. Lord, help me to cultivate gladness, teach me to improve every occasion of receiving mercy from you; so *fill* my mouth with praise and thanksgiving that there may be *no room in it* for anything less choice and precious! I have your dear promise to plead when I ask this, for you have said,

'Open thy mouth wide, and I will fill it.' As the hungry little birds in a nest gape and clamour for the food they need, but cannot obtain for themselves, so do all the emotions of my soul long to be supplied by you with the power to show forth your praise.

Ah, Lord! there is no lack of material for thanksgiving, no dearth of causes for gratitude. There are mountains of mercies to praise you for, seas of exceeding love, boundless stores of grace! I am surrounded, weighed down, covered and submerged with countless blessings, all of which I owe to you, my God. If I could ceaselessly praise you throughout my mortal life, and then through all eternity, I could never begin to repay the debt of love I owe. If every word I spoke, and every act I performed, and every desire of my soul were 'to thy name, and to the remembrance of thee', this would be far less homage, more incomplete devotion than I am bound to render.

Filled . . . with thy honour.' Lord, can it be that *your honour* is thus entrusted to the lips of your believing people? Do you look to such a source for the proclamation of your perfect justice and your glorious grace? Is it in this way that you come seeking 'the fruit of our lips giving thanks to thy name'? How often, then, must we have disappointed and dishonoured you, O Lord! I bow my head for very shame before you, when I think how often you have found upon this tongue of mine either a guilty silence, or thankless and half-hearted words, when there should have been jubilant psalms of praise, and sweetest of songs of thanksgiving. But now, alter all this for me, dear Master: let my mouth be filled with your praise and with your honour *all the day*'. From morning to evening, may the chief thought of my life be, how I shall glorify my God by 'speaking well of his Name'.

Through every moment of every hour of every day, may the consciousness that I am yours, and that you have loved me, stir my spirit to the constant melody of wholehearted gratitude! You have said, 'Whoso offereth praise glorifieth me', and I joyfully reply, 'Yes, Lord! "my lips shall greatly rejoice when I sing unto thee", and your praise shall continually be in my mouth.'

21

The Fetters of Unbelief

*Why could not we cast him out? Jesus said unto them,
Because of your unbelief* (Matt. 17:19–20).

—◦⟨⟩◦—

𝒟EAR LORD, behold another poor failing disciple
comes to you, this morning, with the same pitiful
question! I have tried to live for you, and work for you
– with honest purpose endeavouring to bless others in
your name, yet, how notable and frequent have been
my failures!

Lord, *why could I not* overcome the sin which so easily beset me? *Why could I not* check the sharp word on
my tongue, and subdue the fierce risings of anger in
my heart? *Why can I not* always walk so near to you
that my whole life may be under your sweet control,
and every thought, and deed, and word, be sanctified
by your consent and approval? *Why have I not* the
power to influence and draw others to your dear feet,
that they may find in you, as I have done, 'a very
present help in trouble'?

Lord, I know your answer to me will be the same as
that to your first disciples. Sadly and sorrowfully you
say, *'Because of your unbelief.'*

What a humbling revelation these words convey! My
soul, it is but a little while since you rang the joy-bells
of faith triumphantly! Has your right hand already lost
its skill? Has the wicked unbelief, still lingering within

you stopped the glorious music your faith was making, and turned the happy assertion of 'How shall he not!' into the faithless, whining question of *'How shall he?'* Satan has taunted you with your unworthiness. But do you think your demerit could hold back the hand from blessing which gave 'his only-begotten Son', or overturn the covenant of grace of which he was made 'Surety' in the days of old? Lord, it is too true that my faith is often bound by the fetters of unbelief, and her wings are clipped, so that she can only painfully attempt to fly heavenward. I know this is the secret cause of many an unanswered prayer, many a failure in service and in holy living.

Now I bring myself to you, as much in need of spiritual healing as the poor lunatic boy had of deliverance from demonic possession. Cast out every evil thing, Lord, and manifest in me 'what is the exceeding greatness of thy power to us-ward who believe'. You are the Author and Giver of faith; endue me abundantly with this living grace, banish all doubt and mistrust from my heart, that faith may be always rejoicing, always conquering, always bringing glory to you! 'Lord, I believe; help thou mine unbelief!'

22

The Hill Country of Perfect Trust

Therefore I will look unto the LORD; I will wait for the God of my salvation: my God will hear me (Mic. 7:7).

❧

*H*EART-RENDING griefs are often the forerunners of great spiritual blessing. A heavy wave of affliction is needed which casts some of us high and dry on the safe and sheltered shore of complete confidence in God. It was a most distressful acquaintance with earth's shame and sorrow which drew from the Lord's prophet the exalted utterance of the text, and we often have to learn the blessedness of turning to God, and trusting him, by the sharp pain of finding out that he alone is a dependable and constant Friend.

Come, my heart, God has set you a lesson to repeat, this morning, which has stood you in good stead in many times of sorrow! To say it over again, will help you to learn it by heart, for you cannot too often remember the loving-kindness of the Lord, and the many deliverances he has performed for you.

Reading the first six verses of this chapter, we see in each of them a 'because' for the 'therefore' which follows in the seventh verse. Many and various miseries and woes are here delineated by the prophet. He has discovered the faithlessness of friends, he has endured the pitiless malice of enemies; feuds and factions, bribes and betrayals, crimes and cruelties have surrounded him, even the closest of all human ties has been strained; he is desolate, and discouraged – his soul faints within him; but in the face of all this grief, no, *because* of it, he remembers the Lord, and an upward look to him brings swift and sure relief. The very extremity of his condition has caused him to flee to the only Refuge, the very bitterness of his distresses has suggested the sweet solace of rest in God's unchangeable love.

Dear Father, how often do we, your children, share in the experience so vividly described by Micah! Great tempests of sorrow beat upon us, we see the shipwreck of all our dearest hopes, and suffer the desertion of many friends, before we reach this rock of 'therefore', and can stand upon its summit with uplifted face, regardless of the angry waves below, and with all our hope and expectation centred in God alone. The teaching and the discipline of life are truly blessed to us when earthly troubles serve to raise us nearer to our heavenly Father, and the sad inconstancy of the creature reveals to us more distinctly the immutability of him who has loved us from all eternity.

'Therefore I will look unto the LORD.' Eyes and heart are both sorely aching with grief at the sight of the sin, and selfishness, and sorrow which are within and around me; but help me, dear Lord, to look up, enable

me to 'lift up mine eyes unto the hills, from whence cometh mine help'. As travellers on the great mountains refrain from looking down the steep precipices, keeping their eyes fixed on the heights above lest a sudden vertigo should overcome them, so may I look unto the Lord with humble, steadfast gaze, and receive courage and strength to press onward and upward in the path he has marked out for me!

'*I will wait for the God of my salvation.*' Though bruised and wearied by the roughness of the way, I have at last reached a safe shelter and resting-place where I may wait till my Lord reveals himself to me as my Deliverer.

How blest am I to know that One so mighty both in love and power watches over and directs my steps – One who is not only 'God', but 'the God of *my salvation*'! He has a more tender and personal interest in me than in the angels of heaven, for I am, that marvel of marvels, a sinner saved by grace, a soul redeemed unto God by his most precious blood!

For him I will wait, confident and expectant. As someone lately said, 'I know I am cared for; but just what his care may deem best for me, this I do not know.' I can leave all with him, and wait the unfolding of his will and purpose concerning me.

Waiting for the Lord is often the surest mode of progression in the divine life; and to be silent before him, is not infrequently the most importunate of petitions.

'My God will hear me.' Of course he will; let us never doubt it. This is the language of full assurance, the tongue of the dwellers in the hill country of Perfect Trust. Such speech well becomes those who look to and wait for the God of their salvation.

Dear reader, do *you* use it often and well?

23

Waiting at the Gate

I wait for the LORD, my soul doth wait, and in his word do I hope (Psa. 130:5).

⟨ornament⟩

I AM a suppliant at the door of a palace, a beggar at the gate of a King, but with this gracious dissimilarity to usual petitioners, that the Lord of the palace is my personal Friend, and, though I am waiting outside at present, I possess an invitation to enter, and know that the door will be wide open to me some day. No, more than this, if I tell all that is in my heart – I am daily expecting that the King himself will come and call me in, and admit me to his presence as his own child.

Well, my soul, this is surely a blessed condition of favour and privilege! You may well afford to wait patiently for so glorious a hope as this. You know that *waiting* is far better than *wandering*, and that silently uplifted hands plead more eloquently than a torrent of words. Keep your tarrying, entreating posture; and if the summons come not yet, it should be joy enough to wait and watch for *his* time and *his* will, and to anticipate the coming glory in which he has promised that you shall share.

For what do you say you are waiting? Alms? Entrance? Welcome? You have the first even now, for his bounty reaches you as you stand watching daily at his gates; and the better blessings are certain when he has perfected that which concerns you, for then you will know with glad surprise what he has prepared for the one who waits for him.

Meanwhile, do you not get some wondrous glimpses of your glorious Friend through the lattices, and have there not been times when you caught the sweet tones of his voice as he said, 'I will come again, and receive you unto myself'?

'I wait for the LORD.' Blessed Master, I thank you for my waiting times; they are times of love and favour, they draw me nearer, closer, more urgently to your feet. Your 'delays are not denials'. Your tarryings do but ensure a more abundant providing. When you seem slow to answer prayer, it is but to make me more eager for the mercy, or to teach me to ask with greater confidence, or that you may gather up your blessings in order to bestow them 'exceeding abundantly above all that we ask or think'.

'My soul doth wait.' Ah, Lord! what special blessedness of sweet content I find in waiting before you when you fill my heart with adoring love and gratitude, when I am silent, because no words are needed between you and my wondering soul, when I am humbled to the very dust by your love and favour, yet lifted into the heavenly places through Christ Jesus and thus I wait, and watch, and worship! This is the waiting upon you which renews the strength of my spiritual

life. This is the waiting that never wearies, the expectancy that never disappoints, the 'hope that maketh not ashamed'. Oh, to be found thus waiting *for* God, and *upon* God, 'till he come'!

'And in his word do I hope.' What is his 'word' to you this morning, my soul? Have you already gathered your daily manna, and tasted its sweetness? The heavenly food lies thick around you, for the Lord has strewn the pages of his Word with promises of blessedness to those who wait for him. And remember, his slightest word stands fast and sure; it can never fail you. So, my soul, see that you 'have a promise underneath thee', for then your *waiting* will be *resting*, and a firm foothold for your hope will give you confidence in him who has said, *'They shall not be ashamed that wait for me.'*

24

Absolute Surrender

I am thine, and all that I have (1 Kings 20:4).

A LITTLE WHILE SINCE, dear Lord, you did permit me to sign a contract for the building of a House of Prayer to the honour of your Name. This morning, on the table of my heart there rests another covenant, one I would gladly renew with you, and to which I pray you to set your seal and signature. O my Lord, come near, I beg you; look down with your great love upon me as I write these solemn words, 'I AM THINE, AND ALL THAT I HAVE', and let my soul hear your tender response, 'I have called thee by thy name; thou art mine.'

There is nothing on earth, O Lord, you know, that I desire so much as to be absolutely surrendered to you and to your service. I want the fullest spiritual blessing you can see fit to give me; and to obtain this, I do gladly yield up body, soul, and spirit – all I am and have – into your loving hands, that you may reign over me, and rule within me as my absolute King and Master.

Do you ask me if I have counted the cost? Yes, Lord, it means, 'I am crucified with Christ: nevertheless I live; yet not I, but Christ liveth in me: and the life which I now live in the flesh I live by the faith of the Son of God, who loved me, and gave himself for me.'

This is the cost, but your grace is sufficient to meet it, and to fill your child's heart with joy unspeakable at the thought that she is no longer her own, but 'bought with a price'.

'I am thine.' Who has so great a right to me as you have? Created by you, I belong of necessity to him who made me. Daily preserved by you, the life you maintain ought to be consecrated to your service. But the closest tie of all is that you have loved me, redeemed me from death, purchased me with the price of your own blood, and thus bound me to yourself for ever.

O love amazing and divine, why did you do all this for one so unlovely and unworthy? It is but another instance of 'Even so, Father, for so it seemed good in Thy sight', and, since it has pleased you to be thus gracious, and you have made it possible for me to say, 'I am thine', it must naturally follow that I should add, *'and all that I have'*, laying every possession and power at your dear feet; for what have I, Lord, of anything good or excellent which is not your own gift to me?

I pray you to grant that my surrender may be real, practical, and complete; not in word only, but in deed and in truth, not simply a spiritual submission, which might be counted easy and pleasant, but that constant denial of self and its pleadings, that keeping under of the body, and bringing it into subjection, which I find so difficult to attain.

If you have given me but one talent, may that be so used as to bring the greatest interest of glory to you! My time must not be aimlessly frittered away, or employed for self-indulgence but every hour should bear on its fast flying wings the witness of something said, or done, or thought, for you, my Master, or your service. My money all belongs to you, and every coin of it should be spent, as in your sight, and with your approval. I pray that you would enable me in this matter to render a good account of my stewardship. Deliver me from the evil of looking on gold as a gift, to be used at my will and pleasure, instead of receiving it from you as a sacred loan or trust to be employed and expended only for your glory. Be it much or little which you bestow on me, help me from my heart to say, *'All that I have is thine.'*

O my pitiful Lord, you will remember that my dearest and most precious possession is already in your safe keeping, and that you have long since taught me, by a sorrowful experience, to measure earth's losses by heaven's gain!

Yes, Lord, I can bless you that you have but removed my treasure into your own treasury, and gathered my priceless jewel into your own regalia. 'Of Thine own have I given Thee' when resigning into your arms that most dearly beloved one who is now with you in the glory. Dear Lord, in taking *him*, you seem to have taken ALL THAT I HAVE, so that it is no longer a question of 'surrender', but only of quiet, happy submission, as your will daily unfolds itself, and directs my work and my way.

Lord, keep me ever thus in the secret hiding-place of your love, 'as having nothing, yet possessing all things'; it is so safe a shelter for a weary, waiting soul, and so blessed a way of being made ready for the coming inheritance!

The Life of

SUSANNAH SPURGEON

Charles Ray

CONTENTS

PREFACE

It has been felt that a short biography of Mrs C. H. Spurgeon would be appreciated by the many thousands who have received help through her Book Fund and its auxiliary branches, and by the still greater number of persons who have been incited to increased efforts in the service of Christ through her inspiring example. Mrs Spurgeon was indeed a wonderful woman, and if this little book arouses interest in the Book Fund where hitherto its unique work was unknown, and encourages invalid Christians and others to take up some work for their Master by showing them the power of the weakest, it will have achieved its purpose.

CHARLES RAY
Forest Gate,
Essex,
November 1903

INTRODUCTION

The position of the wife of a great man, and particularly of a great minister, is not only one of rare difficulty but calls for an exercise of unselfishness and self-effacement which is quite contrary to the natural instincts of human nature. The lady who would be a true 'helpmeet' to the popular preacher and God-ordained pastor must to a very large extent sink her own individuality and claims and become absorbed in those of her husband. She must be prepared to part often with the one she loves best on earth, in order that he may go to fulfil his solemn engagements untrammelled by domestic repinings; she must render every assistance in her power and yet not expect to reap the praise from men, which is rightly her due; she must initiate and carry through new plans of Christian effort and be satisfied that they shall be regarded as nothing more than a legitimate part of her husband's ministry; and she must take upon her shoulders a load of responsibility, which the ordinary wife knows nothing of and which amid such a multitude of duties might well overwhelm a strong and vigorous man. If it be true in a general sense, that 'Whoso findeth a wife findeth a good thing and obtaineth favour of the LORD', how much more must it be the case with the minister who is encouraged and helped by his partner in life. The members of the Christian churches little know what they owe to the wives of their pastors and when, by way of faint praise, they oftentimes declare that the lady of the manse has 'done what she could', the expression usually implies a qualification that the work might have been greater or better. How many of those who thus look with a more or less supercilious eye upon the work of the minister's wife do a tenth of the good in the world which can be placed to her credit?

No grander example of the possibilities which the position of a preacher's wife affords, could be offered to her sisters of the manse or to the world at large than Mrs C. H. Spurgeon, whose death on 22nd October, 1903, has left the church poorer than it yet realizes. Called to a position of rare difficulty at an early age, her husband already raised to dazzling heights of popularity, which few could have endured without being lifted up with pride, it was an ordeal for the retiring girl to be thus suddenly thrust into prominence. Then when the storms of abuse and slander broke on her loved one's head, she might well have been crushed and broken, but she bore up and by her words of comfort, her strong affection and her piety and faith, helped him to weather the gale. In every branch of his work she threw her heart and soul, she stinted herself to render financial assistance to the various causes, and to the smallest detail acted with her husband as a faithful steward of the God in whom she trusted. Never did woman fulfil the marriage vow more faithfully.

In sickness and in health, through good report and evil, she was ever his support and it would be difficult to find anywhere another woman who, in spite of adverse circumstances and conditions, ill-health and infirmity, did such monumental work for God and man as Susannah Spurgeon. Her life was one long self-sacrifice. She need not have expended the strength she so much required for herself; no one would have blamed the invalid for seeking comfort in rest, but what she did, she did with a will and as 'unto the Lord'. Her life is a brilliant example of what can be done by a weak woman who devotes herself to the service of the Master, and not only as the wife of Charles Haddon Spurgeon will Mrs Spurgeon live green in the memory of all true Christians, but as herself. As the woman who found solace in suffering by ministering to the needs of others, she will stand out through all time.

Chapter 1

EARLY DAYS

Mrs Spurgeon was born on 15th January, 1832, and her girlhood days were spent partly in the southern suburbs and partly in the City of London, which had not then, as now, ceased to be residential. In the political world the times were stirring; there were wars and rumours of wars, but probably little of the turmoil of the nations was known to the young maiden, for English girls were not then allowed to read morning and evening newspapers and encouraged to give their opinions upon the latest events of the day. Her father, Mr R. B. Thompson, and her mother attended New Park Street Chapel, Southwark, from time to time, and their daughter Susannah used to accompany them, so that with the ministry of the Pastor, James Smith (afterwards of Cheltenham), she was familiar. 'A quaint and rugged preacher, but one well versed in the blessed art of bringing souls to Christ', is how

Mrs Spurgeon describes him. 'Often had I seen him administer the ordinance of baptism to the candidates, wondering with a tearful longing whether I should ever be able thus to confess my faith in the Lord Jesus. I can recall the old-fashioned dapper figure of the senior deacon, of whom I stood very much in awe. He was a lawyer and wore the silk stockings and knee-breeches dear to a former generation. When the time came to give out the hymns he mounted an open desk immediately beneath the pulpit; and from where I sat, I had a side view of him. To the best of my remembrance he was a short, stout man, and his rotund body, perched on his undraped legs and clothed in a long-tailed coat, gave him an unmistakable resemblance to a gigantic robin; and when he chirped out the verses of the hymn in a piping, twittering voice, I thought the likeness was complete!'

Those early experiences at New Park Street Chapel were among the most vivid memories of Mrs Spurgeon's life.

'Well, also', she continues, 'did I know the curious pulpit without any stairs; it looked like a magnified swallow's nest and was entered from behind through a door in the wall. My childish imagination was always excited by the silent and "creepy" manner in which the minister made his appearance therein. One moment the big box would be empty – the next, if I had but glanced down at Bible or hymnbook, and raised my eyes again – there was the preacher, comfortably seated or standing ready to commence the service! I found it very interesting and though I knew there was a matter-of-fact door, through which the good man stepped into his rostrum, this knowledge was not allowed to interfere with, or even explain the fanciful notions I loved to indulge in concerning that mysterious entrance and exit. It was certainly somewhat singular that, in the very pulpit which had exercised such a charm over me, I should have my first glimpse of the one who was to be the love of my heart, and the light of my earthly life.'

The young girl's visits to New Park Street Chapel were no doubt more frequent than they would have been, from the fact that old Mr and Mrs Olney were very fond of her and often invited her to visit them. Naturally on Sundays, during these visits, she usually accompanied Mr and Mrs Olney to the chapel and thus she had more than one association with the place which was to play so large a part in her after-history. Brought up in a godly family and having earnest Christian friends, Susannah Thompson was not indifferent to the importance of religion in the individual life, but it was by means of a sermon from Romans 10:8, 'The word is nigh thee, even in thy mouth, and in thy heart', preached at the old Poultry Chapel, by the Rev. S. B. Bergne, that the girl was first aroused to a sense of her own personal need of a Saviour. 'From that service', she says, 'I date the dawning of the true light in my soul. The Lord said to me, through his servant, "Give me thy heart", and, constrained by his love, that night witnessed my solemn resolution of entire surrender to himself.'

In those days there were no Christian Endeavour Societies, and few attempts at encouraging young converts to engage in service for their Lord. The lack of communion with kindred youthful spirits and the absence of Christian work to occupy the mind and lead to further knowledge of God, were, no doubt, more or less responsible for a state of coldness and indifference which in a short time took the place of the joy and gladness of soul that had followed conversion. 'Seasons of darkness, despondency, and doubt had passed over me,' she says, 'but I had kept all my religious experiences carefully concealed in my own breast', the hesitancy and reserve in this respect being the cause, in Mrs Spurgeon's judgment, of the sickly and sleepy condition of her soul. It was at this juncture that she first came under the influence of the man who was in a few years to become more dear to her than all others.

Chapter 2

FIRST CONTACT WITH
C. H. SPURGEON

On the morning of Sunday, 18th December, 1853, Charles Haddon Spurgeon, then a gauche country youth of nineteen years, preached for the first time in the pulpit of New Park Street Chapel. Susannah Thompson was staying with old Mr and Mrs Olney, but she did not go to the service although like many others the much-talked of experiment of asking a lad from a rural village to occupy the historic pulpit of Benjamin Keach, Dr Gill and Dr Rippon interested her. The members of the Olney family when they returned from the morning service, were full of praise for the preacher, and, in common with others of the congregation, they were determined that in the evening the many empty seats which had obviously discouraged and disconcerted the young minister, should be filled. Friends and acquaintances were called upon and urged to go to New Park Street Chapel, with the result that in the evening the church was full.

Susannah Thompson was there, more to please her friends than herself, for having rigid ideas as to the proprieties of the pulpit, she entertained no pre-possessions in favour of one – and he a mere youth – who dared to break those proprieties. The chapel was filled, a hush fell upon the multitude, and all eyes, including those of the young maiden, were turned towards the pulpit. At last the door in the wall opened and the preacher entered briskly. Miss Thompson was shocked. This was quite contrary to her ideas of what a preacher should be. Young Charles Haddon Spurgeon was evidently from the country; she could have told that in a moment even if she had not known. His clothes had the village tailor marked upon every part of them; round his neck he wore a great stock of black satin, and in his hand he carried a blue handkerchief with white spots! What business had such a youth in the pulpit of Dr Gill and Dr Rippon? And with that thought in her prejudiced mind Susannah Thompson settled down to hear what he had to say.

'Ah!' wrote Mrs Spurgeon in after years, 'how little I then thought that my eyes looked on him who was to be my life's beloved; how little I dreamed of the honour God was preparing for me in the near future! It is a mercy that our lives are not left for us to plan, but that our Father chooses for us; else might we sometimes turn away from our best blessings, and put from us the choicest and loveliest gifts of his providence. For, if the whole truth be told, I was not at all fascinated by the young orator's eloquence, while his countrified manner and speech excited more regret than reverence. Alas, for my vain and foolish heart! I was not spiritually minded enough to understand his earnest presentation of the gospel and his powerful pleading with sinners – but the huge black satin stock, the long badly-trimmed hair, and the blue pocket handkerchief with white spots which he himself has so graphically described – these attracted most of my attention and I fear awakened some feelings of amusement. There was only one sentence of the whole sermon which I carried away with me, and that solely on account of its quaintness, for it seemed to me an extraordinary thing for the preacher to speak of the "living stones in the heavenly temple perfectly joined together with the vermilion cement of Christ's blood".'

When C. H. Spurgeon finally accepted the pastorate of New Park Street Chapel, Miss Thompson often met him at the house of Mr and Mrs Olney, although neither the preacher nor his wife could ever recall their first introduction to one another. The young maiden seems to have soon got over her prejudices and often went to hear the new minister. It was not long before his earnest pleadings aroused her and she realized that her life of indifference and non-service was far front being what it should be.

'Gradually I became alarmed at my back-sliding state and then, by a great effort, I sought spiritual help and guidance from Mr William Olney ('Father' Olney's second son, and my cousin by marriage), who was an active worker in the Sunday School at New Park Street, and a true Mr Greatheart and comforter of young pilgrims. He may have told the new Pastor about me – I cannot say – but one day I was greatly surprised to receive from Mr Spurgeon an illustrated copy of *The Pilgrim's Progress*, in which he had written the inscription "Miss Thompson, with desires for her progress in the blessed pilgrimage, from C. H. Spurgeon, April 20th 1854".

'I do not think', continues Mrs Spurgeon, 'that my beloved had at that time any other thought concerning me than to help a struggling soul heavenward; but I was greatly impressed by his concern for me, and the book became very precious as well as helpful. By degrees, though with much trembling, I told him of my state before God; and he gently led me, by his preaching, and by his conversations, through the power of the Holy Spirit to the cross of Christ for the peace and pardon my weary soul was longing for.'

From this time the intimacy and friendship of the young couple grew, although on Miss Thompson's part, at any rate, there was no thought of love. She tells us, however, that she was happier than she had been since the days at the Poultry Chapel when she was first brought to the feet of Christ, and it is clear that the preacher who had taken London by storm, had proved of real spiritual blessing to this quiet young girl who now sat pretty regularly in his congregation.

Chapter 3

THE DAWNING OF LOVE

The manner and circumstances in which C. H. Spurgeon declared his love to Miss Thompson were very characteristic of the man. At the opening of the Crystal Palace, at Sydenham, on 10th June, 1854, a large party of friends connected with the New Park Street Chapel was present, including the preacher and the young girl to whom he had rendered such valuable spiritual help.

'We occupied some raised seats', says Mrs Spurgeon, 'at the end of the Palace where the great clock is now fixed. As we sat there talking, laughing and amusing ourselves as best we could, while waiting for the procession to pass by, Mr Spurgeon handed me a book into which he had been occasionally dipping, and, pointing to some particular lines said, "What do you think of the poet's suggestion in those verses?" The volume was Martin Tupper's *Proverbial Philosophy*, then recently published, and already beginning to feel the stir of the breezes of adverse criticism which afterwards gathered into a howling tempest of disparagement and scathing sarcasm. No thought had I for authors and their woes at that moment. The pointing finger guided my eyes to the chapter "On Marriage", of which the opening sentences ran thus:

Seek a good wife of thy God, for she is the best gift
    of His providence;
Yet ask not in bold confidence that which He hath
    not promised:
Thou knowest not His good will; be thy prayer
    then submissive thereunto;
And leave thy petition to His mercy assured that
    He will deal well with thee.
If thou art to have a wife of thy youth, she is now
    living on the earth;
Therefore think of her and pray for her weal!

"'Do you pray for him who is to be your husband?" said a soft, low voice in my ear – so soft that no one else heard the whisper.

'I do not remember that the question received any vocal answer; but my fast-beating heart, which sent a tell-tale flush to my cheeks, and my downcast eyes, which feared to reveal the light which at once dawned in them, may have spoken a language which love understood. From that moment a very quiet and subdued little maiden sat by the young Pastor's side, and while the brilliant procession passed round the Palace, I do not think she took so much note of the glittering pageant defiling before her, as of the crowd of newly-awakened emotions which were palpitating within her heart. Neither the book nor its theories were again alluded to, but when the formalities of the opening were over, and the visitors were allowed to leave their seats, the same low voice whispered again, "Will you come and walk round the Palace with me?"

'How we obtained leave of absence from the rest of the party, I know not; but we wandered together for a long time, not only in the wonderful building itself, but in the gardens and even down to the lake, beside which the colossal forms of extinct monsters were being cunningly modelled.'

'During that walk on that memorable day in June, I believe', wrote Mrs Spurgeon, 'a few years before her death, 'God himself united our hearts in indissoluble bonds of true affection, and, though we knew it not, gave us to each other for ever. From that time our friendship grew apace and quickly ripened into deepest love – a love which lives in my heart today as truly, aye, and more solemnly and strongly than it did in those early days; for, though God has seen fit to call my beloved up to higher service, he has left me the consolation of still loving him with all my heart, and believing our love shall be perfected when we meet in that blessed land where Love reigns supreme and eternal.'

Would anyone but Charles Haddon Spurgeon have whispered his love in the midst of a crowd, and have made it known by asking the lady of his choice to pray for her future husband?

Chapter 4

COURTSHIP DAYS

Less than two months after the incident at the Crystal Palace, C. H. Spurgeon formally proposed for the hand of Susannah Thompson. They were in the little old-fashioned garden of the girl's grandfather, with its high brick walls, straight, formal gravel paths and small lawn – 'rather a dreary and unromantic place for a declaration of love', as Mrs Spurgeon described it. 'But,' she says, 'people are not particularly careful as to the selection of their surroundings at such a moment, and do not often take pains to secure a delightful background to the picture, which will for ever be photographed on their hearts. To this day I think of that old garden as a sacred place, a paradise of happiness, since there my beloved sought me for his very own, and told me how much he loved me. Though I thought I knew this already, it was a very different matter to hear him say it, and I trembled and was silent for very joy and gladness.' What words the lover used we are not told, but Mrs Spurgeon has declared that the verbal confession was 'wonderful', and writing forty years afterwards she could ask, 'Was there ever quite such bliss on earth before?' They were one in heart, in soul, in inclination, and even at this stage the great preacher had communicated to his fiancée much of his own spirituality and earnestness. There was more than mere earthly affection in their love for one another, and both felt that indeed the finger of God had marked out a united course for them. 'To me', says Mrs Spurgeon, 'it was a time as *solemn* as it was sweet; and with a great awe in my heart, I left my beloved and, hastening to the house and to an upper room, I knelt before God and praised and thanked him with happy tears for his great mercy in giving me the love of so good a man. If I had known then *how* good he was and how great he would become, I should have been overwhelmed, not so much with the happiness of being his, as with the responsibility which such a position would entail.' In the diary which the young girl kept she thus made a record of that memorable day – August 2nd, 1854, – 'It is impossible to write down all that occurred this morning. I can only adore in silence the mercy of my God, and praise him for all his benefits.'

Miss Thompson now attended New Park Street Chapel pretty regularly, and before long she sought for membership and became a candidate for baptism. The preacher asked her to write out her confession of faith, probably for his own personal perusal only, and this she did in a manner so satisfactory as to elicit a letter from him in which his joy at the work of grace in her soul can scarcely find utterance.

'Oh! I could weep for joy (as I certainly am doing now),' he wrote, 'to think that my beloved can so well testify to a work of grace in her soul. I knew you were *really* a child of God, but I did not think you had been led in such a path. I see my Master has been ploughing deep and it is the deep-sown seed, struggling with the clods, which now makes your bosom heave with distress. If I know anything of spiritual symptoms, I think I know a cure for you. Your position is not the sphere for earnest labour for Christ. You have done all you could in more ways than one; but you are not brought into actual contact either with the saints or with the sinful, sick or miserable, whom you could serve. Active service brings with it warmth and this tends to remove doubting, for our works thus become evidences of our calling and election.

'I flatter no one, but allow me to say, honestly, that few cases which have come under my notice are so satisfactory as yours. Mark, I write not now as your *admiring friend*, but impartially as your Pastor. If the Lord had intended your destruction, he would not have told you such things as these, nor would he enable you so unreservedly to cast yourself upon his faithful promise. As I hope to stand at the bar of God, clear of the blood of all men, it would ill become me to flatter; and as I love you with the deepest and purest affection, far be it from me to trifle with your immortal interests; but I will say again that my gratitude to God ought to be great, as well on my own behalf as yours, that you have been so deeply schooled in the lessons of the heart and have so frequently looked into the charnel-house of your own corruption. There are other lessons to come, that you may be thoroughly furnished; but, oh! my dear one, how good to learn the first lesson well! I loved you once, but feared you might not be an heir of heaven – God in his mercy showed me that you were indeed *elect*. I then thought I might without sin reveal my affection to you – but up to the time I saw your note, I could not imagine that you had seen such great sights and were so thoroughly versed in soul-knowledge. God is good, very good, infinitely good. Oh, how I prize this last gift, because I now know, more than ever, that the Giver loves the gift, and so I may love it too, but only in subservience to him. Dear purchase of a Saviour's blood, you are to me a Saviour's gift, and my heart is full to overflowing with the thought of such continued goodness. I do not wonder at his goodness, for it is just like him, but I cannot but lift up my voice of joy at his manifold mercies.

'Whatever befall us, trouble and adversity, sickness or death, we need not fear a final separation, either from each other or our God. I am glad you are not here just at this moment, for I feel so deeply that I could only throw my arms around you and weep. May the choicest favours be thine, may the Angel of the Covenant be thy companion, may thy supplications be answered, and may thy conversation be with Jesus in heaven!

'Farewell; unto my God and my father's God I commend you. Yours, with pure and holy affection as well as terrestrial love, C. H. Spurgeon.'

Surely a remarkable lover's letter and one which speaks volumes as to the character of both the writer and the recipient. C. H. Spurgeon had said that there were other lessons to come that she might be thoroughly furnished, and this was true not only in her soul's experience, but also in the preparation and schooling for the position of a minister's wife. Some of these lessons, Mrs Spurgeon herself has told us, were far from pleasing, but she learned them well, and became the stronger and more earnest for the teaching. At times the preacher would be so absorbed in his great mission, when about to preach, that on his fiancée entering the vestry, he would fail to recognize her and merely greet her with a handshake as if she were some casual acquaintance or visitor. Once there was a more trying experience still. C. H. Spurgeon was to preach in a large hall at Kennington on a certain afternoon and Miss Thompson accompanied him thither in a cab. The pavement outside the building was thronged with people as were also the entrance hall and staircase leading to the auditorium, and the maiden had hard work in struggling through the mass of people and trying to keep near her lover.

Suddenly he turned in at a side door on the landing, leaving Miss Thompson to manage as best she could in the throng eagerly pressing forward to get into the hall. The burden of souls was resting heavily upon the preacher, and occupied with the momentousness of the message he was to deliver, he had forgotten all about his poor fiancée.

Miss Thompson's feelings at what she considered an unpardonable slight, may easily be imagined. 'At first,' she says, 'I was utterly bewildered, and then, I am sorry to have to confess, I was *angry*.' She at once returned home, without making any further effort to get to a seat, her indignation and grief increasing momentarily. But the young girl possessed that best of gifts, a wise and loving mother, who with the greatest tact sought to soothe her daughter's ruffled spirits.

'She wisely reasoned', says Mrs Spurgeon, 'that my chosen husband was no ordinary man, that his whole life was absolutely dedicated to God and his service, and that I must never, *never* hinder him by trying to, put myself first in his heart. Presently, after much good and loving counsel, my heart grew soft, and I saw I had been very foolish and wilful; and then a cab drew up at the door and dear Mr Spurgeon came running into the house in great excitement, calling, "Where's Susie? I have been searching for her everywhere and cannot find her; has she come back by herself?" My dear mother went to him, took him aside and told him all the truth; and, I think, when he realized the state of things, she had to soothe him also; for he was so innocent at heart of having offended me in any way, that he must have felt I had done him an injustice in thus doubting him. At last, mother came to fetch me to him, and I went downstairs. Quietly he let me tell him how indignant I had felt, and then he repeated mother's little lesson, assuring me of his deep affection for me, but pointing out that, before all things, he was *God's servant*, and I must be prepared to yield my claims to his. I never forgot the teaching of that day; I had learned my hard lesson *by heart*, for I do not recollect ever again seeking to assert my right to his time and attention when any service for God demanded them.'

The incident closed happily with a cosy tea at her mother's house, and Mrs Spurgeon speaks of the sweet calm which reigned in the hearts of all after the storm of the afternoon. When a few weeks later the preacher was to fulfil an engagement at Windsor he wrote and asked his fiancée to accompany him, adding, 'Possibly, I may be again inattentive to you if you do go; but this will be nice for us both – that Charles may have space for mending, and that 'Susie' may exhibit her growth in knowledge of his character, by patiently enduring his failings.'

In April 1855, Miss Thompson paid a week's visit to Colchester in company with her fiancé, to be introduced to his parents and family. It was a very happy holiday, the fact that the lovers were together all day, and that the Rev. John Spurgeon and his wife 'welcomed and petted' their future daughter-in-law, being the principal contributory causes. When the young minister was in London he had little time for courtship, and when he did visit his fiancée at her Brixton home he usually took proofs of a sermon with him to revise for the press. 'I learned to be quiet and to mind my own business while this important work was going on', says Mrs Spurgeon. 'It was good discipline for the Pastor's intended wife.'

Even in these early days, C. H. Spurgeon was abused in the press, and he found some consolation in writing to his fiancée, who did much to comfort and sustain him.

'I am down in the valley,' he says, in a letter of May 1855, 'partly because of two desperate attacks in the *Sheffield Independent* and the *Empire*, and partly because I cannot find a subject. Yet faith fails not. I know and believe the promise and am not afraid to rest upon it. All the scars I receive are scars of honour; so, faint heart, on to the battle! My love, were you here, how you would comfort me; but since you are not I shall do what is better still, go upstairs alone and pour out my grief into my Saviour's ear.'

About this time Miss Thompson's parents removed from Brixton to Falcon Square in the City of London, and the lovers saw more of one another, than they had hitherto done. The young maiden commenced to help her future husband in his literary work and very proud she was of the honour and trust thus implied, although the responsibility seemed at first overwhelming.

His wonderful popularity and success as a preacher naturally delighted and awed the timid maiden, but with the pleasure was mingled something of anxiety and distress, for the strain on the preacher's physical power when addressing the large congregations that gathered at Exeter Hall was tremendous, and his fiancée, sitting watching him from the body of the Hall, often felt she must rush to his succour. 'A glass of Chilli vinegar', she says, 'always stood on a shelf under the desk before him, and I knew what to expect when he had recourse to that remedy. Oh, how my heart ached for him! What self-control I had to exercise to appear calm and collected and keep quietly in my seat up in that little side gallery! How I longed to have the *right* to go and comfort and cheer him when the service was over! But I had to walk away, as other people did – I who belonged to him and was closer to his heart than anyone there!

It was severe discipline, for a young and loving spirit.'

When the preacher went to Scotland in July 1855, his first long journey by rail, he wrote many letters to his fiancée, giving her an account of the services he conducted, and the crowds who flocked to hear him, and asking her to pray that he might be sustained and helped, and his preaching blessed to the souls of the people. 'I shall feel deeply indebted to you,' he says in one note, 'if you will pray very earnestly for me. I fear I am not so full of love to God as I used to be. I lament my sad decline in spiritual things. You and others have not observed it but I am now conscious of it; and a sense thereof has put bitterness in my cup of joy. Oh! what is it to be popular, to be successful, to have abundance, even to have love so sweet as yours – if I should be left of God to fall and to depart from his ways? I tremble at the giddy height on which I stand, and could wish myself un-known, for indeed, I am unworthy of all my honours and my fame. I trust I shall now commence anew and wear no longer the linsey-woolsey garment; but, I beseech you, blend your hearty prayers with mine, that two of us may be agreed, and thus will you promote the usefulness and holiness and happiness of one whom you love.'

His affection for the maiden of his choice grew deeper, if that were possible, during this absence.

'I have had daydreams of you while driving along', he writes in one letter. 'I thought you were very near me. It is not long, dearest, before I shall again enjoy your sweet society, if the providence of God permits. I knew I loved you very much before, but now I feel how necessary you are to me; and you will not lose much by my absence, if you find me, on my return, more attentive to your feelings, as well as equally affectionate. I can now thoroughly sympathize with your tears, because I feel in no little degree that pang of absence which my constant engagements prevented me from noticing when in London. How then must you, with so much leisure, have felt my absence from you even though you well knew that it was unavoidable on my part! My darling, accept love of the deepest and purest kind from one who is not prone to exaggerate, but who feels that here there is no room for hyperbole.'

It must have been no ordinary woman who could draw such letters from Charles Haddon Spurgeon.

Chapter 5

MARRIED LIFE

The wedding of Susannah Thompson and Charles Haddon Spurgeon took place at New Park Street Chapel on January 8th, 1856, Dr Alexander Fletcher of Finsbury Chapel officiating. As may be imagined in the case of a man whose name was in everybody's mouth, and whose remarkable work was the topic of discussion up and down the country, it was quite impossible for the wedding to be a quiet one. At a very early hour in the morning people began to gather outside the Chapel, ladies being among the first arrivals, and soon after eight o'clock the crowd had swelled to such proportions, that New Park Street and some adjoining thoroughfares were blocked with people, and traffic was practically at a standstill. A special body of police had to be summoned to prevent accidents. When the chapel doors were at last opened, there was a rush for seats, and in less than half an hour the building was filled to its utmost extent. Large numbers who had tickets of admission but arrived late were unable to gain entrance. Many went home when they found that there was no chance of their being able to get inside the chapel, but some thousands still remained in the streets to see the bride and bridegroom enter and leave.

It must have been a trying ordeal for the modest and retiring girl. She had risen early and spent much time in her bedroom in private prayer. Although awed with a sense of the responsibilities which she was about to assume, she was 'happy beyond expression' that the Lord had so favoured her, and on her knees, with no one else near, she earnestly sought strength and blessing and guidance in the new life opening before her.

The dressing for the ceremony did not take an unconscionable time, as it does with some maidens, for Susannah Thompson was very simply attired, and as she drove through the city to the chapel with her father the young girl's chief thought was, 'as the passers-by cast astonished glances at the wedding equipage whether they all knew what a wonderful bridegroom she was going to meet'. The crowds standing in the streets adjoining New Park Street, bewildered the bride, and she remembered little more until she was inside the building, 'a large wedding party in the table-pew, dear old Dr Alexander Fletcher beaming benignly on the bride and bridegroom before him, and the deacons endeavouring to calm and satisfy the excited and eager onlookers.'

The service was commenced by the congregation singing the hymn, 'Salvation, O, the joyful sound!' after which Dr Fletcher read the hundredth Psalm and prayed for the divine blessing upon the young couple. The venerable minister then gave a short address and the wedding ceremony was performed in the usual manner. The reading of another lesson, a hymn sung by the congregation and a closing prayer, completed the proceedings, and Mr and Mrs Spurgeon, after receiving the congratulations of their friends in the chapel, drove away amid the loud and continued cheering of the crowds gathered outside the building.

A brief honeymoon of ten days was spent in Paris, and as Mrs Spurgeon had often been to that city before and was a good French scholar, she acted as cicerone [guide] to her husband. Together they visited the various churches and palaces and museums, the lady finding a new interest in all these familiar places on account of 'those loving eyes that now looked upon them' with her. Years afterwards during one of C. H. Spurgeon's frequent visits to the French capital he wrote to his wife, 'My heart flies to you as I remember my first visit to this city under your dear guidance. I love you now as then, only multiplied many times.' The happy couple would have liked to prolong the holiday, but the preacher was unable to leave his work, and so they returned to their first united home – a modest house in New Kent Road, London, where as in all their future homes, the best room became the library. 'We never encumbered ourselves', says Mrs Spurgeon, 'with what a modern writer calls "the draw-back of a drawing-room", perhaps for the good reason that we were such homely, busy people that we had no need of so useless a place – but more especially, I think, because the best room was always felt to belong by right to the one who "laboured much in the Lord". Never have I regretted this early decision; it is a wise arrangement for a minister's house, if not for any other.'

Housekeeping was commenced on a very modest scale, for C. H. Spurgeon was keenly anxious to provide a training for young preachers who needed a course of education to fit them for the ministry, and his wife threw herself into the work with a zeal not less than his own. She was a splendid manageress, and by means of rigid economies quite a substantial amount was saved towards the support and education of the first student, the success of this effort leading to the foundation of the Pastors' College.

'I rejoice', says Mrs Spurgeon, 'to remember how I shared my beloved's joy when he founded the Institution, and that together we planned and pinched in order to carry out the purpose of his loving heart; it gave me quite a motherly interest in the College, and "our own men". The chief difficulty with regard to money matters in those days was to "make both ends meet"; we never had enough left over to "tie a bow and ends"; but I can see now that this was God's way of preparing us to sympathize with and help poor pastors in the years which were to come.'

There were times when the devoted couple abstained from almost necessary things in order to have money to help on the work, and to the young wife it must have been truly a period of anxiety when 'means were sorely straitened and the coffers of both College and household were well-nigh empty'. But there were joys which more than compensated for any cares of this kind. What times of happiness were spent in the little home on Sunday evenings after the duties of the day were done. On his return from Chapel tired by his labours the preacher would enjoy a light repast and then throw himself into an easy chair by the fireside, while his wife sat on a low cushion at his feet reading to him from the pages of George Herbert or some other Christian poet. Or, if the young minister felt that he had not been as earnest in his preaching as he should have been, the poet would give place to Baxter's *Reformed Pastor,* and as the solemn words were read, husband and wife would sob and weep together, he 'from the smitings of a very tender conscience towards God', and she because she 'loved him and wanted to share his grief'.

The constant absence from home of Charles Haddon Spurgeon in fulfilment of his preaching engagements were sources of sore trial to the young wife. Often tired of waiting in the sitting-room late at night for his return, she would pace up and down the passage, praying that he might be brought back in safety to his home, and with what a thrill of joy and thankfulness did she open the door and welcome him, when his step was heard outside.

Once and once only she broke down, when her dear one was about to leave in the early morning for a distant mission, and the tears could not be kept back. 'Wifey,' said her husband, 'do you think that when any of the children of Israel brought a lamb to the Lord's altar as an offering to him they stood and wept over it when they had seen it laid there?' and when she replied in the negative he added, tenderly, 'Well, don't you see, you are giving me to God in letting me go to preach the gospel to poor sinners, and do you think he likes to see you cry over your sacrifice?'

'Could ever a rebuke have been more sweetly and graciously given?' says Mrs Spurgeon. 'It sank deep into my heart, carrying comfort with it and thenceforward when I parted with him, the tears were scarcely ever allowed to show themselves, or if a stray one or two dared to run over the boundaries he would say, "What! crying over your lamb, wifey?" and this reminder would quickly dry them up, and bring a smile in their place.'

One very remarkable incident happened about this time. On a certain Saturday evening, C. H. Spurgeon found himself quite unable to get any light upon the text from which he believed he ought to preach on the following morning. Commentaries were consulted, but in vain, and his wife could not help him. The rest of the story shall be told in Mrs Spurgeon's own words.

'He sat up very late and was utterly worn out and dispirited, for all his efforts to get at the heart of the text were unavailing. I advised him to retire to rest and soothed him by suggesting that if he would try to sleep then, he would probably in the morning feel quite refreshed and able to study to better purpose. "If I go to sleep now, wifey, will you wake me very early so that I may have plenty of time to prepare?" With my loving assurance that I would watch the time for him and call him soon enough, he was satisfied; and, like a trusting, tired child, he laid his head upon the pillow and slept soundly and sweetly at once.

'By-and-by a wonderful thing happened. During the first dawning hours of the Sabbath, I heard him talking in his sleep, and roused myself to listen attentively. Soon I realized that he was going over the subject of the verse which had been so obscure to him, and was giving a clear and distinct exposition of its meaning with much force and freshness. I set myself with almost trembling joy to understand and follow all that he was saying, for I knew that if I could but seize and remember the salient points of the discourse he would have no difficulty in developing and enlarging upon them. Never preacher had a more eager and anxious hearer! What if I should let the precious words slip? I had no means at hand of "taking notes", so, like Nehemiah, "I prayed to the

God of heaven", and asked that I might receive and retain the thoughts which he had given to his servant in his sleep, and which were so singularly entrusted to my keeping. As I lay repeating over and over again the chief points I wished to remember, my happiness was very great in anticipation of his surprise and delight on awaking; but I had kept vigil so long, cherishing my joy, that I must have been overcome with slumber just when the usual time for rising came, for he awoke with a frightened start, and seeing the tell-tale clock, said, "Oh, wifey, you said you would wake me very early, and now see the time! Oh, why did you let me sleep? What shall I do? What shall I do?" "Listen, beloved," I answered; and I told him all I had heard. "Why! that's just what I wanted," he exclaimed; "that is the true explanation of the whole verse! And you say I preached it in my sleep?" "It is wonderful", he repeated again and again, and we both praised the Lord for so remarkable a manifestation of his power and love.'

Chapter 6

A DARK SHADOW

On 20th September 1856, twin sons were born to Mrs Spurgeon at her home in the New Kent Road, and the joy of husband and wife knew no bounds. Fortunately the event fell upon a Saturday, and C. H. Spurgeon was able to remain indoors from morning to night. With what pride he gazed upon the babes, and how tenderly he comforted his wife and spoke of the new and happy responsibility which they now had to fulfil! The boys were named Charles and Thomas, and from the first there was a tacit understanding and desire that they should be devoted to the service of God. No cloud that could mar the happiness and joy of the home seemed visible, and there was a holy peace brooding over the little family for which husband and wife repeatedly and devoutly thanked their Lord.

But suddenly and without warning, when things seemed at their brightest, the black shadow of a dreadful sorrow was cast over the young and happy lives, and the faith of the wife and mother must have been such as that which the prophets of old possessed or she would have been distraught.

Exactly a month had elapsed since the birth of her boys. She was still very weak although able to leave her room, and on a certain Sunday evening, was lying upon the couch in the little sitting room of her home. That evening, 19th October 1856, was to become a terrible memory in the lives of husband and wife, but at that time no dread was entertained, at any rate on the part of Mrs Spurgeon, and there was every prospect that her husband was to have another of those triumphs in the service of his Master which had followed in constant succession since his advent to London.

The young minister was to preach for the first time in the Surrey Gardens Music Hall, where, later in the evening, owing to the machinations of evil-disposed persons, a scene of death and desolation resulted.[1] There had been prayer at home, and with his wife's parting benediction, the young minister set out for the Hall. She lay at home thinking of the great task and praying that the Lord would bless his

[1] A false report of fire was raised and in the ensuing panic seven of those present were killed and almost thirty injured.

message to the assembled thousands. Then her mind reverted to her children: 'I was dreaming of all sorts of lovely possibilities and pleasures,' says Mrs Spurgeon, 'when I heard a carriage stop at the gate. It was far too early for my husband to come home and I wondered who my unexpected visitor could be. Presently one of the deacons was ushered into the room, and I saw at once, from his manner, that something unusual had happened. I besought him to tell me all quickly and he did so, kindly, and with much sympathy; and he kneeled by the couch and prayed that we might have grace and strength to bear the terrible trial which had so suddenly come upon us. But how thankful I was when he went away! I wanted to be alone, that I might cry to God in this hour of darkness and death! When my beloved was brought home he looked a wreck of his former self – an hour's agony of mind had changed his whole appearance and bearing. The night that ensued was one of weeping and wailing and indescribable sorrow. He refused to be comforted. I thought the morning would never break; and when it did come it brought no relief.

'The Lord has mercifully blotted out from my mind most of the details of the time of grief which followed when my beloved's anguish was so deep and violent that reason seemed to totter in her throne, and we sometimes feared he would never preach again. It was truly "the valley of the shadow of death" through which we then walked; and, like poor Christian, we here "sighed bitterly" for the pathway was so dark that ofttimes when we lifted up our foot to set forward, we knew not where or upon what we should set it next.'

The story of the disaster at the Music Hall is too well-known to need any description here, but how many women in Mrs Spurgeon's delicate condition could have borne the terrible trouble as she did, and not only have fulfilled the duties of a mother but proved a comfort and stay to her husband in his mental anguish?

C. H. Spurgeon was taken by friends to Croydon where he stayed in the house of Mr Winsor, one of his deacons, and Mrs Spurgeon with the babies joined him there. It was hoped that the rest and the change of scene would aid in the restoration of his mental equilibrium, and although at first his spirit seemed to be imprisoned in darkness, light at last broke in. 'We had been walking together as usual' (in the garden), says Mrs Spurgeon, 'he restless and anguished; I, sorrowful and amazed, wondering what the end of these things would be; when at the foot of the steps which gave access to the house, he stopped suddenly, and turned to me, and, with the old sweet light in his eyes (ah! how grievous had been its absence!), he said, "Dearest, how foolish I have been! Why! what does it matter what becomes of me, if the Lord shall but be glorified?" – and he repeated with eagerness and intense emphasis, Philippians 2:9–11: "Wherefore God also hath highly exalted him and given him a name which is above every name: that at the name of Jesus every knee should bow, of things in heaven, and things in earth and things under the earth, and that every tongue should confess that Jesus Christ is Lord to the glory of God the Father." "If Christ be exalted," he said – and his face glowed with holy fervour – "let him do as he pleases with me; my one prayer shall be, that I may die to self and live wholly for him and for his honour; Oh, wifey, I see it all now! Praise the Lord with me!'"

The husband having recovered his peace of mind, and the wife being strengthened in body, it was decided, while at Croydon, to dedicate the twin sons to the Lord and his service. A number of friends were invited, and the time was spent in prayer and praise, the babies being carried round the room at the conclusion, so that they might be kissed and blessed by those present. Surely those prayers have been answered many times over in the lives of Charles and Thomas Spurgeon.

The Music Hall disaster called forth the virulent abuse of a certain section of the Press, and the preacher collected the newspaper comments and criticisms, as indeed he did throughout his career, and handed them to his wife who stuck them in a book, on the cover of which C. H. Spurgeon himself wrote the title, 'Facts, Fiction and Facetiae'. Late in life the devoted wife could smile as she read the unjust and cruel words written by her husband's enemies, 'but at the time of their publication what a grievous affliction these slanders were to me', she says. 'My heart alternately sorrowed over him and flamed with indignation against his detractors. For a long time I wondered how I could set continual comfort before his eyes, till, at last, I hit upon the expedient of having the following verses printed in large old English type and enclosed in a pretty Oxford frame: "Blessed are ye when men shall revile you and persecute you and shall say all manner of evil against you falsely for my sake. Rejoice and be exceeding glad: for great is your reward in heaven: for so persecuted they the prophets which were before you' – Matthew 5:11–12. The text was hung up in our own room and was read over by the dear preacher every morning, fulfilling its purpose most blessedly, for it strengthened his heart and enabled him to buckle on the invisible armour, whereby he could calmly walk among men, unruffled by their calumnies, and concerned only for their best and highest interests.'

Chapter 7

HAPPINESS AND SERVICE

In 1857 Mr and Mrs Spurgeon moved to Helensburgh House, Nightingale Lane, Clapham, a place which they found far more congenial than their first home in the New Kent Road. Clapham was at that time quite a rural district and, as the house possessed a large garden, the preacher greatly enjoyed the quiet and retirement which he could find there, in the midst of his abundant labours. The country lanes, too, provided delightful walks where the young couple could take recreation without being followed or accosted by admirers, which was not always the case in the neighbourhood of their old residence. Speaking of the garden, Mrs Spurgeon says: 'Oh, what a delightsome place we thought it, though it was a very wilderness through long neglect – the blackberry bushes impertinently asserting themselves to be trees, and the fruit trees running wild for want of the pruning knife. It was all the more interesting to us in this sweet confusion and artlessness because we had the happy task of bringing it gradually into accord with our ideas of what a garden should be. I must admit that we made many absurd mistakes both in house and garden management in those young days of ours; but what did that matter? No two birds ever felt more exquisite joy in building their nest in the fork of a tree-branch than did we in planning and placing, altering and rearranging our pretty country home.'

Here, from time to time, a number of distinguished persons visited the minister and his wife, and here, during an illness of the preacher, much pleasant intercourse was had with John Ruskin, who, on one occasion, carried to the house as a present for his friends some charming engravings and some bottles of wine of a rare vintage. Mrs Spurgeon speaks eloquently of the delightful times spent in her rural Clapham home. 'We lived', she says, 'in the dear old house in Nightingale Lane for many happy years; and looking back upon them from this distance of time, I think they must have been the least shadowed by care and sorrow of all the years of our married life. We were both young and full of high spirits. We had fairly good health, and devoutly loved each other. Our children grew apace in the sweet country air, and my whole time and strength were given to advance my dear husband's welfare and happiness. I deemed it my joy and privilege to be ever at his side, accompanying him on many of his preaching journeys, nursing him in his occasional illnesses, his delighted companion during his holiday trips, always watching over and tending him with the enthusiasm and sympathy which my great love for him inspired. 'I mention this,' she explains, 'not to suggest any sort of merit on my part, but simply that I may here record my heartfelt gratitude to God that, for a period of ten blessed years, I was permitted to encircle him with all the comforting care and tender affection which it was in a wife's power to bestow. Afterwards God ordered it otherwise. He saw fit to reverse our position to each other; and for a long season, suffering instead of service became my daily portion, and the care of comforting a sick wife fell upon my beloved.'

The garden was a regular rendezvous of songbirds, and during her periods of convalescence it was Mrs Spurgeon's delight to sit at the window and feed the little creatures. In this way she made many feathered friends, and the birds would hop around her and feed from her hand, perfect love having quite cast out fear.

Saturday mornings for a good many years were devoted to the students, who used to march down from Mr Rogers' house, where they resided, to Nightingale Lane, and there in the garden listen to the addresses of C. H. Spurgeon on theology, preaching and kindred topics, which were really the foundation of the famous *Lectures to My Students*.

While she enjoyed good health Mrs Spurgeon took an active part in the work of her husband's church, both at New Park Street Chapel and afterwards at the Metropolitan Tabernacle. She attended the services, often gave spiritual consolation to women and girls who were in trouble about their souls, and assisted the female candidates at the baptismal services. Writing in the *British Banner*, on 12th April 1861, of the first service of this kind in the mammoth building that had just been opened, Dr Campbell said:

'The interest of the thing was overpowering. We doubt if it was a whit inferior to that of taking the veil in the Church of Rome. There was the young orator, the idol of the assembly, in the water with a countenance radiant as the light, and there, on the pathway, was Mrs Spurgeon, a most prepossessing young lady – the admiration of all who beheld her – with courtly dignity and inimitable modesty, kindly leading forward the trembling sisters in succession to her husband, who gently and gracefully took and immersed them with varied remark and honied phrase, all kind, pertinent to the occasion, and greatly fitted to strengthen, encourage and cheer.'

When, about a month later, the first church-meeting was held in the Tabernacle and a record of thanks and gratitude to God was placed on the pages of the Church-book, Mrs Spurgeon was the first of a long list of members to sign it after the names of the pastor, deacons and elders had been appended.

Chapter 8

HUSBAND AND WIFE

Mrs Spurgeon, in the earlier years of her married life, used to accompany her husband in his holidays both in England and on the Continent, but in 1868, she tells us, her travelling days were done. 'Henceforth for many years I was a prisoner in a sick-chamber, and my beloved had to leave me when the strain of his many labours and responsibilities compelled him to seek rest far away from home. These separations were very painful to hearts so tenderly united as were ours, but we each bore our share of the sorrow as heroically as we could and softened it as far as possible by constant correspondence.' And what a delightful correspondence it was – love letters of the very best and highest kind.

'God bless you,' wrote the husband on one occasion, 'and help you to bear my absence. Better that I should be away well, than at home suffering – better to your loving heart, I know. Do not fancy, even for a moment, that absence could make our hearts colder to each other; our attachment is now a perfect union, indissoluble for ever. My sense of your value and experience of your goodness are now united to the deep passion of love which was there at the first alone. Every year casts out another anchor to hold me even more firmly to you, though none was needed even from the first. May my own Lord, whose chastening hand has necessitated this absence, give you a secret inward recompense in soul and also another recompense in the healing of the body! All my heart remains in your keeping.'

'Did I but know that you are better,' he writes on another occasion, 'I don't think I should have more to wish except your company', and a day or two later, 'God be thanked for even the twinkling stars of better news in the letter I have just received from your dear self.' In a letter from Rome, we find the passage: 'I had two such precious letters from you this morning, worth to me far more than all the gems of ancient or modern art. The material of which they are composed is their main value, though there is also no mean skill revealed in its manipulation. They are pure as alabaster, far more precious than porphyry or verd-antique; no mention shall be made of malachite or onyx, for love surpasses them all.'

Charles Haddon Spurgeon looked upon the writing of these letters as more than a loving duty to his wife. Knowing how pressed he was with other correspondence that had to be attended to, and with literary work, she often used to urge him to write less often to her, so as to get more rest for himself, but this he would not hear of, and except when taking a long railway journey, he used to write a letter to his wife every day that he was absent from her. 'Every word I write', he says in one note, 'is a pleasure to me, as much as ever it can be to you; it is only a lot of odds and ends I send you, but I put them down as they come, so that you may see it costs me no labour, but is just a happy scribble. Don't fret because I write you so many letters; it is such a pleasure to tell out my joy.' At another time, when sending some pen and ink sketches which he had made of the women's head-dresses in Italy, he writes, 'Now, sweetheart, may these trifles amuse you; *I count it a holy work to draw them*, if they cause you but one happy smile.'

'That I smiled on them then, and weep over them now', said Mrs Spurgeon a year or two ago, referring to these sketches and the letter that accompanied them, 'is but a natural consequence of the more complete separation which God has willed for us – he, dwelling in the land of glory – I, still tarrying amid the shadows of earth – but I verily believe that when I join him, "beyond the smiling and the weeping", there will be tender remembrances of all these details of earthly love and of the plenitudes of blessings which it garnered in our united lives. Surely we shall talk of all these things in the pauses of adoring worship and of joyful service. There must be sweet converse in heaven between those who loved and suffered and served together here below. Next to the rapture of seeing the King in his beauty and beholding the face of him who redeemed us to God by his blood, must be the happiness of the communion of saints in that place of inconceivable blessedness which God has prepared for them that love him.'

Those partings of husband and wife, after the latter became an invalid, must have been sore wrenches to Mrs Spurgeon's heart but, in accordance with the resolution she had made before and at marriage, she never faltered, but gave her loved one up willingly for service or for those continental holidays which were necessary for his health. 'I thank God', she said late in life, 'that he enabled me to carry out this determination and rejoice that I have no cause to reproach myself with being a drag on the swift wheels of his consecrated life. I do not take any credit to myself for this; it was the Lord's will concerning me, and he saw to it that I received the necessary training whereby in after years I could cheerfully surrender his chosen servant to the incessant demands of his ministry, his literary work, and the multiplied labours of his exceptionally busy life.'

That this was no vain and empty boast was clearly confirmed by a letter which C. H. Spurgeon wrote to his wife in 1871, in which he declared, 'None know how grateful I am to God for you. In all I have ever done for him you have a large share, for in making me so happy you have fitted me for service. Not an ounce of power has ever been lost to the good cause through you. I have served the Lord far more and never less for your sweet companionship.'

Chapter 9

MIDDLE LIFE

After the preacher and his wife had been living in Helensburgh House, Nightingale Lane, for close upon a dozen years, the building was found altogether too small and inconvenient for a man whose work needed a very large library and consequently much space to store his books. The old house was loved for its happy associations by both husband and wife, but, realizing the need for a more commodious dwelling, it was, after due consideration, decided to pull down the building and erect a new Helensburgh House which should meet the altered and increased needs of the preacher and his wife. The demolition took place in 1869, and on the site arose a handsome house with ample room for all the requirements of its owners. Mr and Mrs Spurgeon had always been lavishly generous with their money, and had at all times given every available pound that they possessed to one or other of the great causes which they had at heart. A few of their wealthier friends therefore came to the conclusion that it would be unfair to let them be saddled with the cost of the new house, which was only rendered a necessity because of the unselfish labours and extraordinary energy of the pastor in ever increasing his efforts for good, and these friends determined to defray the principal part of the cost as a token of their esteem and appreciation. Mr William Higgs, the builder of the Metropolitan Tabernacle, built the new Helensburgh House, and no efforts were spared to make it a worthy gift and a suitable dwelling for the devoted minister and his invalid wife.

Some time before the building was ready for occupation, the preacher met the donors, and Mrs Spurgeon, who had been staying at Brighton since the demolition of her old home, came up to London in order to be present at the gathering. C. H. Spurgeon made a dainty little speech, thanking his kind friends for their gift and paying a loving tribute to their generosity. 'My wife and I', he concluded, 'have firmly resolved that we will never go into debt for anything, yet you know something of the continuous claims upon us in connection with the work of the Lord', and he explained that the reason why he was not rich was that he refused to avail himself of many opportunities of acquiring wealth, such as by a lecturing trip to America, when he could have obtained more money in a few weeks than he was likely to receive through his ministry in many years. 'There is no intent on my part to rest now that I have a new house. If possible, I shall work harder than ever before and preach better than ever', and all that the speaker uttered for himself, he declared, his wife re-echoed.

After this interesting meeting, Mrs Spurgeon, who was a great sufferer at the period, went back to Brighton, where Sir James Young Simpson of Edinburgh performed a difficult operation upon her that had the effect of giving her some relief from pain and resulted in a slightly better state of health. Meanwhile her husband took upon himself the whole duty of furnishing and preparing the new house for habitation. How lovingly he did this work, and how carefully he sought to please his wife in all that he performed, the following letter which Mrs Spurgeon received will show:

'My Own Dear Sufferer – I am pained indeed to learn from T.'s kind note that you are still in so sad a condition. Oh, may the ever-merciful God be pleased to give you ease! I have been quite a long round today – if a "round" can be "long". First to Finsbury to buy the wardrobe – a beauty. I hope you will live long to hang your garments in it, every thread of them precious to me for your dear sake. Next to Hewlett's for a chandelier for the dining-room. Found one quite to my taste and yours. Then to Negretti and Zambra's to buy a barometer for my own very fancy, for I have long promised to treat myself to one. On the road I obtained the Presburg biscuits, and within their box I send this note, hoping it may reach you the more quickly. They are sweetened with my love and prayers.

'The bedroom will look well with the wardrobe in it; at least, so I hope. It is well made, and, I believe, as nearly as I could tell, precisely all you wished for. Joe [Mr Joseph Passmore had given this as a present] is very good, and should have a wee note whenever darling feels she could write it without too much fatigue; but not yet. I bought also a table for you in case you should have to keep your bed. It rises or falls by a screw, and also winds sideways, so as to go over the bed, and then it has a flap for a book or paper, so that my dear one may read or write in comfort while lying down. I could not resist the pleasure of making this little gift to my poor suffering wifey, only hoping it might not often be in requisition, but might be a help when there was a needs-be for it. Remember, all I buy, I pay for. I have paid for everything as yet with the earnings of my pen, graciously sent me in time of need. It is my ambition to leave nothing for you to be anxious about. I shall find the money for the curtains, etc., and you will amuse yourself by giving orders for them after your own delightful taste.

'I must not write more; and, indeed, matter runs short except the old, old story of a love which grieves over you and would fain work a miracle and raise you up to perfect health. I fear the heat afflicts you. Well did the elder say to John in Patmos concerning those who are before the throne of God, "Neither shall the sun light on them nor any heat." – Yours to love in life and death, and eternally, C. H. S.'

When everything was ready, Mrs Spurgeon's health for a time forbade her returning from Brighton, and her husband had to inhabit the house alone. But when at last she could take up her abode once again in Nightingale Lane she found that the loving care of her husband had forgotten nothing that could in any way conduce to the comfort of an invalid almost entirely confined to her couch. 'Never', she wrote, 'will the rapture with which he welcomed her home be forgotten, nor the joyful pride with which he pointed out all the arrangements he had made so that her captivity should have every possible compensation and alleviation. There was a cunningly contrived cupboard in one corner of the room into which he had gathered all the details of his loving care for her. When the doors were opened, a dainty washing apparatus was disclosed with hot and cold water laid on, so that no fatigue in ascending and descending the stairways should be necessary, and even the towels were embroidered with her name. He had thought of *everything*; and there were such tender touches of devoted love upon all the surroundings of the little room that no words can describe her emotions when first she gazed upon them, and afterwards when she proved by practical experience their exceeding usefulness and value.'

During her sad illness at this time, Mrs Spurgeon had one very remarkable instance of a desire of hers being granted by what cannot but be accepted as a divine interposition. Her husband often used to ask if there were anything she would like him to get for her. The usual answer was a negative. But one day in a half-bantering tone she said, 'I should like an opal ring and a piping bullfinch!'

Her husband was surprised, but replied, 'Ah, you know I cannot get those for you!' For several days the curious request was laughed over, and then it passed from the memories of both husband and wife. Mrs Spurgeon herself shall tell the sequel of the story.

'One Thursday evening, on his return from the Tabernacle, he (the preacher) came into my room with such a beaming face and such love-lighted eyes, that I knew something had delighted him very much. In his hand he held a tiny box, and I am sure his pleasure exceeded mine as he took from it a beautiful little ring and placed it on my finger. "There is your opal ring, my darling", he said, and then he told me of the strange way in which it had come. An old lady whom he had once seen when she was ill, sent a note to the Tabernacle to say she desired to give Mrs Spurgeon a small present, and could someone be sent to her to receive it. Mr Spurgeon's private secretary went accordingly and brought the little parcel, which, when opened, was found to contain this opal ring. How we talked of the Lord's tender love for his stricken child and of his condescension in thus stooping to supply an unnecessary gratification to his dear servant's sick one, I must leave my readers to imagine; but I can remember feeling that the Lord was very near to us.

'Not long after that I was moved to Brighton, there to pass a crisis in my life, the result of which would be a restoration to better health, or death. One evening, when my dear husband came from London, he brought a large package with him, and, uncovering it, disclosed a cage containing a lovely piping bullfinch! My astonishment was great, my joy unbounded, and these emotions were intensified as he related the way in which he became possessed of the coveted treasure. He had been to see a dear friend of ours, whose husband was sick unto death, and after commending the sufferer to God in prayer, Mrs T. said to him, "I want you to take my pet bird to Mrs Spurgeon; I would give him to none but her; his songs are too much for my poor husband in his weak state, and I know that 'Bully' will interest and amuse Mrs Spurgeon in her loneliness while you are so much away from her." Mr Spurgeon then told her of my desire for such a companion, and together they rejoiced over the care of the loving heavenly Father, who had so wondrously provided the very gift his child had longed for. With that cage beside him the journey to Brighton was a very short one, and when "Bully" piped his pretty song and took a hemp seed as a reward from the lips of his new mistress, there were eyes with joyful tears in them and hearts overflowing with praise to God in the little room by the sea that night, and the dear Pastor's comment was, "I think you are one of your heavenly

Father's spoiled children, and he just gives you whatever you ask for."

'Does anyone doubt that this bird was a direct love-gift from the pitiful Father?' asks Mrs Spurgeon. 'Do I hear someone say, "Oh! it was all 'chance' that brought about such coincidences as these"? Ah, dear friends, those of you who have been similarly indulged by him know of a certainty that it is not so. He who cares for all the works of his hand cares with infinite tenderness for the children of his love, and thinks nothing which concerns them too small or too trivial to notice. If our faith were stronger and our love more perfect, we should see far greater marvels than these in our daily lives.'

Although so weak and ailing and confined to her bedroom for such long periods of time, Mrs Spurgeon was a faithful trainer of her twin sons in the Christian doctrine, and she had the joy of seeing them both brought to the Lord at an early age. 'I trace my early conversion', Pastor Thomas Spurgeon has written, 'directly to her earnest pleading and bright example. She denied herself the pleasure of attending Sunday evening services that she might minister the Word of Life to her household. There she taught me to sing, but to mean it first –

I do believe, I will believe,
    That Jesus died for me;
That, on the cross, He shed His blood
    From sin to set me free.

'My dear brother was brought to Christ through
the pointed word of a missionary; but he, too, gladly
owns that mother's influence and teaching had their
part in the matter. By these, the soil was made ready
for a later sowing.'

On 21st September 1874, the sons were baptized
by their father at the Metropolitan Tabernacle in the
presence of an immense concourse of people, and
Mrs Spurgeon was herself an eyewitness of this open
confession of faith made by her boys. On that occasion she was presented by the church with an
illuminated address, in which hearty thanks were
expressed 'to Almighty God for calling so early in
life to the fellowship of the saints the two sons of
our beloved and honoured pastor', and praising 'our
gracious Lord that it should have pleased him to use
so greatly the pious teachings and example of our
dear sister, Mrs Spurgeon, to the quickening and
fostering of the divine life in the hearts of her twin
sons, and we earnestly pray', concluded the address,
'that amidst her long-continued sufferings she may

ever be consoled with all spiritual comfort and by the growing devoutness of those who are thus twice given to her in the Lord.'

Chapter 10

FOUNDING OF THE BOOK FUND

M rs Spurgeon, had she organized no new work herself, would always have been remembered as the wife of the great preacher to whom she rendered such valuable help and encouragement and who, to repeat C. H. Spurgeon's own words, was indeed as 'an angel of God' to him. But, apart from any such associations and the reflected glory from her husband, Mrs Spurgeon's name deserves to live for ever in the annals of the Christian church in connection with her fund for supplying theological books to clergymen and ministers too poor to buy them.

As a branch of Christian effort this work was, and is, quite unique, and its vast importance and necessity to the ministry and to the church at large, cannot be overestimated. In his preface to Mrs Spurgeon's volume, *Ten Years of My Life in the Service of the Book Fund*, the pastor of the Tabernacle expressed his conviction 'that the work was sadly needed, has been exceedingly useful, and is still urgently called for'. 'How can many of our ministers buy books?' he asked. 'How can those in the villages get them at all? What must their ministries become if their minds are starved? Is it not a duty to relieve the famine which is raging in many a manse? Is it not a prudential measure, worthy of the attention of all who wish to see the masses influenced by religion, that the preachers who occupy our pulpits should be kept well furnished with material for thought?' Incredible as it may seem, the state of things revealed when the Book Fund was started was so bad that many ministers had been unable to buy a new book for ten years. 'Does anybody wonder if preachers are sometimes dull?' was C. H. Spurgeon's comment on this fact.

Like most other important works, the Book Fund grew from a very simple beginning, and there was no idea at the first of the wonderful way in which the movement would develop. In the summer of 1875 Mr Spurgeon completed the first volume of his *Lectures to My Students*, and, having given a proof copy to his wife, asked her what she thought of the book. 'I wish I could place it in the hands of every minister in England', was the reply, and the preacher at once rejoined, 'Then why not do so: how much will you give?' This was driving the nail home with a vengeance. Mrs Spurgeon was not prepared for such a challenge, but she began to wonder if she could not spare the money from her housekeeping or personal account. It would necessitate pressure somewhere, she knew, for money was not plentiful just then. Suddenly a flash of memory made the whole way clear. 'Upstairs in a little drawer were some carefully hoarded crown pieces, which, owing to some foolish fancy, I had been gathering for years whenever chance threw one in my way; these I now counted out and found they made a sum *exactly* sufficient to pay for one hundred copies of the work. If a twinge of regret at parting from my cherished but unwieldy favourites passed over me, it was gone in an instant, and then they were given freely and thankfully to the Lord, and in that moment, though I knew it not, the Book Fund was inaugurated.

The next number of *The Sword and the Trowel*, that for July 1875, contained an announcement of Mrs Spurgeon's intention, and inviting poor Baptist ministers to apply for the book. The applications proved far more numerous than was anticipated, and although she could not supply all demands, the generous donor distributed two hundred copies of the book instead of the one hundred which she had at first proposed. In *The Sword and the Trowel* for August, C. H. Spurgeon referred to the matter again and said, 'It has been a great pleasure to our beloved wife to give a book to so many needy servants of the Lord; but it is a sad fact that there should be so many needing such a present. Cannot something be done to provide ministers with books? If they cannot be made rich in money, they ought not for the people's sake to be starved in soul.' This appeal had due effect, and friends began to forward money, so that by the following month (September) parcels of books were being sent out to ministers every day, and the work was formally designated 'Mrs Spurgeon's Book Fund'.

A gentleman contributed a number of good books for distribution among the poor ministers, and other people, who were unable to send money, followed his example and gave volumes from their libraries. Of course, the acceptance and acknowledgment of gifts in kind led to a good deal of rubbish being sent to Mrs Spurgeon, who several times had to gently protest against worthless volumes, fit only for the rag-shop, being 'presented' to the Book Fund. 'I really fear', she wrote in one report, 'that some people think that *anything in the shape of a book* will do for a minister, or they would scarcely send such things as *Advice to Mothers*, or *Letters to a Son*, as aids to pulpit preparation.'

On another occasion she wrote: 'There are in this pleasant world of ours many kind and tender-hearted people who, after perusing the report of my Book Fund, straightway rush off to their bookcases and in an enthusiasm of goodwill pull down a pile of old books and pack them off to me for my poor pastors, in the full belief that they have thus rendered the best possible service to the Fund and the Fund's Manager and the Fund's Manager's needy folk. I should be very sorry to damp any kindly ardour or seem ungrateful for proofs of willing sympathy, but I feel constrained to point out as tenderly as possible to my well-meaning but mistaken friends that such presents are worse than useless to me. I am often puzzled how to get rid of the encumbrances which were meant to be blessings! Usually when good people thus disturb the dusty solitude of their bookshelves the result is as follows: A large number of volumes of *The Evangelical Magazine* and *The Baptist Record*, musty perhaps and always incomplete; some ancient *Sermons* by the venerable pastor they "sat under" half a century ago, a book or two of *Poems* by "nobody knows who", a few old works on some abstruse notions, a *French Grammar and Exercises*, Magnall's *Questions*, *Advice to a Newly Married Pair*, and – I was going to say – a *Cookery Book*, but I think that might be an exaggeration where all else is simple, earnest fact. Now, what could my poor pastors care for rubbish such as this?' C. H. Spurgeon himself, in acknowledging in his magazine the first gift of valuable books from the gentleman above-mentioned, said, 'We have on several occasions in days past received parcels consisting of old magazines and the sweepings of libraries, and we have concluded that the donors thought we kept a butter shop, but this friend has sent really standard volumes, which will, we trust, be a boon to some poor preacher.'

During the autumn Mrs Spurgeon became seriously ill and the distribution of books had to be delayed, but by November she had sufficiently recovered to commence work again, and scarcely a day went by but what some poor minister was made happy by receiving a gift of volumes which his slender means would never have allowed him to purchase. No distinction as to denomination was made, and although the poverty of Baptist ministers was perhaps more acute than that of others, yet there were hundreds of preachers in all the churches quite unable to purchase the books which they absolutely needed for their work. It was not long before the valuable volumes of *The Treasury of David* were added to the *Lectures*, and gradually other books were distributed, mostly C. H. Spurgeon's own writings and sermons, as these were generally asked for by the poor ministers applying. By January, 1876, without any solicitation, friends had sent in £182, and this had increased in August, one year after the inauguration of the Fund, to upwards of £500, representing a distribution of 3,058 volumes. By a generous arrangement of the publishers of C. H. Spurgeon's works, the books were supplied for purposes of the Fund at a very low rate, so that £500 in money would purchase about £800 worth of books.

The novel and important work was now established on a solid and permanent basis, and the interest in the movement to furnish poor ministers' libraries was increasing. Quoting from the letters of recipients, who expressed their intense joy and thankfulness at receiving the books, Mrs Spurgeon wrote in *The Sword and the Trowel* after the first twelve months' work: 'Now this is very beautiful and admirable, but is there not also something most sorrowfully suggestive to the church of God? Surely these "servants of Christ", these "ambassadors for God", ought to have received better treatment at our hands than to have been left pining so long without the aids which are vitally necessary to them in their sacred calling. Books are as truly a minister's needful tools as the plane and the hammer and the saw are the necessary adjuncts of a carpenter's bench. We pity a poor mechanic, whom accident has deprived of his working gear, we straightway get up a subscription to restore it, and certainly never expect a stroke of work from him while it is lacking; why, I wonder, do we not bring the same commonsense help to our poor ministers, and furnish them liberally with the means of procuring the essentially important books? Is it not pitiful to think of their struggling on from year to year on £100, £80, £60, and some (I am ashamed to write it) on less than £50 per annum? Many have large families, many more sick wives, some, alas! have both; they have heavy doctors' bills to pay, their children's education to provide for, are obliged to keep up a respectable appearance, or their hearers would be scandalized; and how they manage to do all this and yet keep out of debt (as, to their honour and credit be it said, the majority of them do), only they and their ever-faithful God can know! I never hear a word of complaint from them, only sometimes a pathetic line or two like this: "After upwards of sixteen years' service in the Master's vineyard I am sorry to say that, with a small salary and a wife and five daughters to provide for, my library is exceedingly small, and I am not in a position to increase its size by purchasing books." Or, again, like this: "My salary is small (£60), and if I did not get some little help from some benevolent societies, I should have very great difficulty in keeping the wolf from the door." Are these men to be kept in poverty so deep that they positively cannot afford the price of a new book without letting their little ones go barefoot? "The labourer is worthy of his hire", but these poor labourers in the gospel field get a pittance which is unworthy both of the workman and the work, and if their people (who ought to help them more) either cannot or will not do so, we at least, dear friends, will do all in our power to encourage their hearts and refresh their drooping spirits. This is a digression, I daresay from my authorized subject, but I was obliged to say what I have said, because my heart was hot within me, and I so earnestly want to do these poor brethren good service.'

Mrs. Spurgeon took as her motto the words which her husband put into the mouth of the spendthrift in *John Ploughman's Talk*: 'Spend and God will send', and before the Book Fund was nine months old she had a remarkable proof of her faith being honoured. A gentleman sent £50 for the Fund, the largest gift received up to that time, and it was quickly distributed in the form of books. About six months later the same gentleman (who insisted upon remaining anonymous to everyone else) called upon Mrs Spurgeon and declared his intention of giving to every one of the five hundred Calvinistic Methodist ministers, preachers, and students in North Wales, through the Book Fund, a copy of *Lectures to My Students*, and at the same time he handed over another sum of £50 to meet expenses. Before the distribution in North Wales was completed, the same generous donor gave authority to Mrs Spurgeon to continue at his expense the despatch of copies to the ministers and preachers in South Wales.

Chapter 11

THE BOOK FUND GROWS

A few months before the Book Fund originated, Mrs Spurgeon had sown in a large garden flower pot some lemon pips, hoping that one at least of them would spring up and grow into a healthy plant. Sure enough, one did take root, and a frail stem with two tiny leaves made its appearance, and was tenderly cared for by its owner. In a happy moment Mrs Spurgeon's mind associated her Book Fund, then a 'tender plant', whose continued existence might be precarious, but which had splendid possibilities in it, with the little lemon tree, and as the latter flourished and increased, she determined to regard it as something in the nature of an augury of the prosperity of her Fund, each leaf representing a sum of a hundred pounds, which sooner or later would surely come to hand. The growth of the tree was steady and continuous, and, curiously enough, the Fund kept pace with it. As fresh leaves were formed, so new subscribers came forward to help on Mrs Spurgeon's labour of love, and all through their history the Book Fund and the lemon tree were associated in the mind of the lady to whom they were both so dear.

Although subscriptions were not solicited, there was no lack of funds. Between August 1876, and January 1877, no less than £926 was received, and by the end of the second year more than £2,000 had come in and been expended. The progress of time only served to show how widespread was the need, and the letters which Mrs Spurgeon received by the score each week formed pathetic reading, whilst the gratitude expressed by recipients of books was quite painful in its intensity.

She had been trained in her husband's school of faith, and it was to God and not to man that she looked both for the money to carry on her mission and for the health and strength to enable her to cope with the ever growing work of correspondence and organization. 'The Book Fund has been nourished and fed from the King's Treasury,' she wrote in 1877, 'and I must "make my boast in the Lord" that all needful supplies for the carrying on of the work have plainly borne the stamp of heaven's own merit. I say this because I have never asked help of anyone but him, never solicited a donation from any creature, yet money has always been forthcoming and the supplies have constantly been in due proportion to the needs. Once only during the year did the Lord try my faith by allowing the grants of books to out-number the gifts of money, and then it was only for a "small moment" that a fear overshadowed me. The dark cloud very speedily passed away, and fresh sup-plies made me more than ever satisfied with the resolution I had formed to draw only on the unlim-ited resources of my heavenly Treasurer. None of the friends whose hearts have "devised liberal things" on behalf of my work will reproach me with ingratitude towards them when I lay my *first* loving thanks at his feet; they will rather join me in praising him for so sweetly inclining their hearts to help his needy ones, and will joyfully say, "O Lord, of Thine own have we given thee."

'I recall with very glad satisfaction the first don-ation which reached me "for sending books to ministers". It came anonymously, and was but five shillings' worth of stamps, yet it was very precious, and proved like a revelation to me, for it opened up a vista of possible usefulness and exceeding bright-ness. The mustard seed of my faith grew forthwith into a "great" tree, and sweet birds of hope and expectation sat singing in its branches. "You'll see", I said to my boys, "the Lord will send me hundreds of pounds for this work." For many a day afterwards mother's "hundreds of pounds" became a "household word" of good-humoured merriment and badinage. And now "the Lord has made me to laugh", for the hundreds have grown into thousands. He has done "exceeding abundantly above what I could ask or even think", and faith, with such a God to believe in and depend upon, ought surely to smile at impossibilities and say "it shall be done."'

The work which Mrs Spurgeon had undertaken did not for very long confine itself exclusively to the supply of books. At the beginning of 1877 a friend placed at her disposal a sum of money from which she could draw such amounts as were necessary for the relief of poor ministers in dire financial straits, and, her husband and other friends adding to this sum, a very useful and much-needed Pastors' Aid Fund was founded, which has proved a valuable auxiliary and supplement to the Book Fund. At the end of the year, too, a number of Christian ladies undertook to supply warm garments and other suitable clothing for the families of poor pastors, and this branch of the work has also gone on increasing to the present time. Still another advance was made when two friends provided the means for sending *The Sword and the Trowel* regularly for a year to each of sixty ministers who could not afford to purchase a religious magazine for themselves. Perhaps these developments of Mrs Spurgeon's original idea were foreshadowed by the announcement which the gardener made to her some time earlier: 'Your lemon tree is brought up to the house, ma'am. It is making a great deal of new wood.'

In 1878, Mrs Spurgeon's malady reached an acute stage, and indeed so serious was her condition that her son Thomas, who was then in Australia, received an urgent cable to return at once. For some time her life was despaired of, but the crisis was passed successfully, and, although still an invalid, she was able once again to give all her attention to the Book Fund. The work, however, did not diminish on account of the illness, for the arrears were soon made up and the year was the most successful since the inauguration. Those periods of pain and weariness which Mrs Spurgeon was called upon to suffer never led her to despair or to rebel against the strange providence that had so marked out a hilly path for her. If for a moment the mystery of life perplexed her, she quickly found comfort and consolation by trusting to him who does all things well. Her diaries or notebooks contain many entries which tell of her experiences of soul during the most trying periods of her life. Referring to this time of crisis she writes: 'At the close of a very dark and gloomy day I lay resting on my couch as the deeper night drew on, and though all was bright within my cosy little room, some of the external darkness seemed to have entered into my soul and obscured its spiritual vision. Vainly I tried to see the hand which I knew held mine and guided my fog-enveloped feet along a steep and slippery path of suffering. In sorrow of heart I asked, "Why does my Lord thus deal with his child? Why does he so often send sharp and bitter pain to visit me? Why does he permit lingering weakness to hinder the sweet service I long to render to his poor servants?" These fretful questions were quickly answered, and though in a strange language, no interpreter was needed save the conscious whisper of my own heart.

'For a while silence reigned in the little room, broken only by the crackling of an oak log burning on the hearth. Suddenly I heard a sweet, soft sound, a little, clear, musical note, like the tender trill of a robin beneath my window. "What *can* it be?" I said to my companion, who was dozing in the firelight; "surely no bird can be singing out there at this time of the year and night!" We listened, and again heard the faint plaintive notes, so sweet, so melodious, yet mysterious enough to provoke for a moment our undisguised wonder. Presently my friend exclaimed, "It comes from the log on the fire!!" and we soon ascertained that her surprised assertion was correct. The fire was letting loose the imprisoned music from the old oak's inmost heart. Perchance he had garnered up this song in the days when all went well with him, when birds twittered merrily on his branches, and the soft sunlight flecked his tender leaves with gold; but he had grown old since then and hardened; ring after ring of knotty growth had sealed up the long-forgotten melody until the fierce tongues of the flames came to consume his callousness and the vehement heat of the fire wrung from him at once a song and a sacrifice.

'Oh! thought I, when the fire of affliction draws songs of praise from us, then indeed are we purified and our God is glorified! Perhaps some of us are like this old oak log – cold, hard and insensible; we should give forth no melodious sounds were it not for the *fire* which kindles round us, and releases tender notes of trust in him, and cheerful compliance with his will. As I mused the fire burned and my soul found sweet comfort in the parable so strangely set forth before me. Singing in the fire! Yes, God helping us if that is the only way to get harmony out of these hard, apathetic hearts, let the furnace be heated seven times hotter than before.'

How the suffering wife had caught the spirit and faith of her husband, who, in *his* sufferings, later on, wrote words almost to the same effect as the foregoing!

The story of the Book Fund in its financial department during these early days, and indeed up till the present, is very much like that of the Stockwell Orphanage or the Pastors' College, on a small scale. Unsolicited, the money would come in from the most unexpected sources just when it was needed, and would be spent without delay in the full and faithful expectation that more would follow to take its place. An entry in Mrs Spurgeon's notebook a month or two after that which records the message of the burning oak log says, 'My heart praises and extols the goodness of the Lord, and my hand shall at once record the mercy which, like a blessed rain on a thirsty land, has so sweetly refreshed my spirit. This afternoon a constant and generous friend brought £100 for the Book Fund. This was cause for devout thankfulness and great joy, for lately an unusually large number of books has been going out week by week though funds have flowed in less freely. But it was not till a few hours after receiving this noble donation that I saw fully the Lord's tender care and pitying love in sending me this help *just when* he knew I should most sorely need it. By the late post that night came my quarterly account for books, and so heavy was it that, in fear and haste I turned to my ledger to see the available balance, and with an emotion I shall not easily forget, I found that, but for the gift of £100 a few hours previously, I should have been £60 in debt. Did not the Father's care thus keep the sparrow from falling to the ground? A sleepless night and much distress of spirit would have resulted from my discovery of so serious a deficit in my funds, but the Lord's watchful love prevented this. "Before I called he answered", and though trouble was not very distant, he had said, "It shall not come nigh thee." O my soul, bless thou the Lord and forget not this his loving "benefit"! A tumult of joy and delight arose within me as I saw in this incident, not a mere chance or a happy combination of circumstances, but the guiding and sustaining hand of the loving Lord, who had most certainly arranged and ordered for me this pleasant way of comfort and relief. "I am poor and needy, yet the Lord thinketh upon me." A fresh revelation of his wonderful love seemeth to be vouchsafed to my soul by this opportune blessing and a cheque became "an outward and visible sign of an inward and spiritual grace".

'I hastened to my dear husband that he might share my joy, and I found in him a willing listener to the sweet "old story" of his Master's grace and power. Then, after a word or two of fervent praise to God on my behalf, he wrote the following letter to the friend by whose liberal hand our gracious God had sent this notable deliverance:

'Dear friend, – I should like you to know why you were sent here this afternoon, and what an angel of mercy you were to my dear wife and so to me. The Lord bless you. Soon after you were gone my wife's quarter's bill for books came in for £340, and she had only £280 apart from your cheque. Poor soul! she has never spent more than her income before, and if you had not come, I fear it would have crushed her to be £60 in debt. How good of the Lord to send you in the nick of time! We joined our praises together, and we do also very gratefully join our prayers for you. God bless you, and make up to you your generous gifts above all your own desires. I could not refrain from telling you this; it is one of the sparkling facts which will make happy memories to help to stay our faith in future trials if they come again. God bless you. – Yours heartily, C. H. Spurgeon.

Exactly a week after the above entry in Mrs. Spurgeon's diary we find another of similar purport. '£20 from a *new* friend to-day! My heart keeps whispering, "Indulgent God, how kind!" At the beginning of this week I had hesitated about sending my usual order for books, having less in hand than would justify a large increase of stock, but I ventured, and lo! the Lord has sent me all I need for present wants, and with it a firm assurance to my soul that "those who trust in him shall never be ashamed."'

Money now began to be received in considerable sums. Gifts of twenty-five and fifty pounds from single individuals were by no means uncommon, and from the great Silver Wedding Testimonial presented by the Tabernacle Church to C. H. Spurgeon the Book Fund received £100, and the Pastors' Aid Fund another £100.

Of course there were disappointments, but the trials only increased the faith. Thus after losing an expected bequest of £200, Mrs Spurgeon wrote: 'A legacy of £200 left to the Book Fund by an old and much loved friend becomes null and void in consequence of legal inaccuracies in the will; and thus though the dear deceased's tender remembrance of me is inalienable, I lose the splendid help to my beloved work which she intended should partly alleviate my grief at her departure and in some measure compensate for the cessation of her constant loving aid. I try to bear my disappointment bravely and sink my own sorrow in sympathy with the President in the far heavier loss sustained in like manner by the Pastors' College, and though I felt at first to some extent "bowed down" by the unexpected failure of my promised good fortune, I am since upholden and comforted exceedingly, for I know that "the Lord is able to give me much more than this", and this puts all thought of murmuring from me, and enables me to look up again from human help to that infinitely more certain portion with which the Lord supplies all my need as it arises. Perhaps I needed such a lesson, and shall do well to learn it off "by heart". It is quite possible that I felt too elated on hearing of the generous bequest and counted up my riches with somewhat of carnal pride mingling with the gratification which was allowable; certain it is that I once reckoned upon a grand total at the end of the year quite eclipsing all former amounts, and it may be that the Lord saw this was not good for me, and that the reception of too much "treasure laid up on earth" would have disturbed and imperilled that lovely posture of constant dependence on my God which he has taught me to delight in, and has so graciously honoured and rewarded. I think also I may learn from this untoward event to bless and praise him more humbly and heartily for his grand and immutable "will" and that "his ways are not our ways".'

After her own comparative recovery in 1879, Mrs Spurgeon's husband fell ill, and had to go to the South of France, whence frequent bulletins were cabled giving news of his condition to the anxious wife at home. The work of the Book Fund, however, kept her from brooding over her sorrow. A notebook entry in December says, 'Blessed be God! Better news comes now. The telegrams have ceased and letters written with unsteady pen by poor pained hands, yet inexpressibly precious, have arrived. In this trying time hard work has been a benefactor to me, for the urgency of the daily correspondence admits of no comfortable nursing of grief, and Book Fund management knows no cessation while the Lord sends so many needy applicants.'

The gifts were not confined to poor preachers in Great Britain, although naturally the majority of parcels were distributed in the homeland. But many a missionary has been helped in his work by a grant from the Book Fund, and native preachers in the West Indies, Africa, and elsewhere, have participated in the benefits of the Fund.

In June 1879, the Bishop of Sierra Leone, Dr Cheetham, who had heard of the good work which Mrs Spurgeon had instituted and was carrying on, called upon her at Helensburgh House and solicited the gift of *The Treasury of David* for one of his coloured pastors. Mrs Spurgeon readily promised to give these books, and also some others, and the Bishop before he left enrolled his name as a donor to the Fund. In Jamaica the gifts of books were greatly appreciated by both the English missionaries and the native pastors.

Chapter 12

CONTINUED SUCCESS OF THE BOOK FUND

To give anything like a history of Mrs Spurgeon's Book Fund in these pages is quite out of the question. Those who wish for a detailed account of how the work grew and thrived and developed year after year will find it in the volumes of reports which Mrs Spurgeon herself prepared, *Ten Years of My Life* and *Ten Years After*. That the work did grow and did thrive and did develop a comparison of the statistics for succeeding twelve-months will clearly show. Thus in 1881 the number of volumes distributed was 7,298, and 10,517 single sermons by C. H. Spurgeon were sent off in parcels for free distribution. In 1883 the books for the year had increased to 11,351; in the following year the number stood at 9,149 and the sermons at 11,981, whilst three years later the annual distribution included 10,311 volumes and 21,227 sermons. The numbers have varied in the different years since that time according to the state of the finances, and owing to the growing infirmity of Mrs Spurgeon the work has receded somewhat from its high-water mark of 1883. The last report issued by her, that for the years 1901 and 1902, showed that 10,113 volumes had been distributed during the two years, and that in the twenty-seven years since the Fund was started a total of 199,315 valuable theological works had been put into the hands of ministers, preachers and missionaries too poor to purchase them. It is indeed a marvellous record of service done by an invalid lady, and to find a parallel would be difficult.

The whole of the work entailed by the Book Fund and its branch organizations was attended to by Mrs Spurgeon personally, and some idea of how heavy was the correspondence alone, may be gathered from the fact that the average number of letters received per month was about five hundred, and in two periods of four weeks each the numbers were 657 and 755 respectively. Nor was the work all composed of 'pleasant fruit and flowers', for, as Mrs Spurgeon tells us, in referring to the fact that her lemon tree had developed a few sharp thorns, there were in connection with the Book Fund 'some thorns concealed here and there which wound the hand that inadvertently touches them.' Some ministers, whose behaviour showed either that they greatly misunderstood the nature of the Book Fund or that their characters were strangely out of keeping with their office, would write in such a strain as practically amounted to a demand for books whilst others quite ignored the conditions on which the volumes were given and loftily declined to say whether their incomes were under the £150 per annum, which was laid down as the limit. One man, who had requested a grant without saying anything: as to his financial condition, when asked kindly whether his income brought him within the sphere of the work, replied angrily, 'Permit me to say I have no wish to be considered a *pauper*.'

'Ever since the Master gave me this charge to keep,' wrote Mrs Spurgeon when mentioning the above incident, 'he knows I have tried to minister in gentle, kindly fashion to his servants, but occasionally the spirit of my service is overlooked by them, and my gifts are either claimed as a right or disdained as a charity. Few and far between are these ugly thorns on my beautiful tree; tender and loving acknowledgments of my work are the rule and when an exception comes I can well afford to forgive and forget it. Were it not that a chronicler is required to be faithful and give fairly both sides of the history he is writing, I should have left unrecorded this painful part of a most pleasant and blessed service.

It is truly wonderful that being so often prostrated, Mrs Spurgeon was able to keep the Book Fund in so flourishing a condition. Over and over again she was completely laid aside, and when once more convalescent her weakness was such that none but a woman whose whole being was given up to service for the Lord could have sustained the mental and physical stress of such a great work.

In his preface to *Ten Years of My Life*, the substantial profits from which, owing to the generosity of the authoress and publishers, were given to the Book Fund, C. H. Spurgeon wrote: 'I gratefully adore the goodness of our heavenly Father in directing my beloved wife to a work which has been, to her, fruitful in unutterable happiness. That it has cost her more pain than it would be fitting to reveal is most true; but that it has brought her a boundless joy is equally certain. Our gracious Lord ministered to his suffering child in the most effectual, manner when he graciously led her to minister to the necessities of his servants. By this means he called her away from her personal griefs, gave tone and concentration to her life, led her to continual dealings with himself, and raised her nearer the centre of that region where other than earthly joys and sorrows reign supreme. Let every believer accept this as the inference of experience: that for most human maladies the best relief and antidote will be found in self-sacrificing work for the Lord Jesus.' The writer went on, however, to say that his wife's increasing weakness was not equal to continuing the work at its present increasing rate.

'From this date the beloved worker feels that she must slacken. The business has overpowered her: the wagon is running over the horse. A measure of this ministry *must* pass into other hands, for, to my great sorrow, I have seen that overpressure is now causing a growing sense of weariness. It cannot long be possible to wake up every morning with a dread of that pile of letters; to sit all day with scarce an interval, writing and bookkeeping; and to go to bed at night with a sigh that the last stroke has hardly been made before the eyes have closed. However brave an invalid may be, love will not always allow such incessant toil to grind down a willing spirit. As the embodiment of loving prudence I feel that I must place an urgent veto upon the continuance of this labour *at its present rate*.' But although there was a slight diminution in the work, Mrs Spurgeon remained at her post, and with the exception of one period in the year 1888, when she was so seriously ill that her severe physical suffering deprived her of all ability to continue her labours or even to open her letters, she carried on the Book Fund to the end of her life. Often the persistent and steady labour taxed her energy to its utmost limit, but the work was done and done well.

No distinction as to church or creed was made in the distribution of books, and the 25,000 or more ministers who have benefited by the Fund up to the present time include some belonging to the Church of England, the Baptists, the Congregationalists, all kinds of Methodists, the Presbyterians, the Moravians, the Society of Friends, the Unitarians, the Irvingites, the Waldensians, the Nestorians, the Plymouth Brethren, the Lutherans, the Sweden-borgians, the Countess of Huntingdon's Connexion, and the Morisonians, besides a very large number of evangelists and missionaries.

In the earlier days of the Fund's history it was always a grief to Mrs Spurgeon that she was unable to accede to the pathetic requests for books made by poor local preachers, as the applications from regular ministers were more than sufficient to absorb all her grants. She mentioned this matter in her report for 1887, and, after quoting from a letter, said: This is a real cry for help; will it not touch the heart of any who can respond to it?' The appeal did touch the heart of a willing worker, Mr Sydney S. Bagster, of the Conference Hall, Mildmay Park, who organized a successful Auxiliary Book Fund for the free distribution of theological works among poor lay preachers. The work of sending off parcels commenced on May 1st, 1888, and by the end of that year 126 preachers had received 1,142 volumes. Mr Bagster continued to carry on the Auxiliary Book Fund until 1891, when it was handed over to Mrs Spurgeon, and became a part of the regular work carried on at her home. On an average, about sixteen hundred volumes have been distributed annually among the poor local preachers up to the present time.

As year followed year there were increasing developments, which added to the labours of the devoted founder of the Book Fund. The monthly grant of copies of *The Sword and the Trowel*, already referred to, assumed large proportions. Many thousands of C. H. Spurgeon's sermons and other pamphlets were sent out each year to preachers both at home and abroad, and there has been for a long time past a Fund for General Use in the Work of the Lord which bore the expense of the translation of C. H. Spurgeon's sermons into foreign languages and their publication, as well as supplying help to preachers and others in need, to chapels handicapped by a debt, and various missions needing monetary assistance.

The Pastors' Aid Fund became an established institution, and each year Mrs Spurgeon was able to distribute an average of over three hundred pounds among the pastors and their families who had needs more pressing than ordinary. The grants of bonnets, shawls, and other articles of clothing has also been an important offshoot and auxiliary of the Book Fund.

Up to the last Mrs Spurgeon regarded her lemon tree with a rare affection as being a remarkable symbol of her work. At the conclusion of the volume, *Ten Years After*, she wrote: 'The great central stem is, metaphorically, the *Book Fund* itself, out of which all the branches have naturally grown, and with which they all continue to be vitally connected. Springing from the main trunk, and almost rivalling it in strength and usefulness, is the largest limb of the tree, which represents the *Pastors' Aid Fund*. This, in its turn, has thrown out the widely spreading branch from which the well-filled boxes of the *'Westwood'*

Clothing Society have dropped into many a poor pastor's home. Peering between the thickly interlaced foliage I spy a sturdy bough bearing the inscription *Home Distribution of Sermons*, and an equally vigorous offshoot dedicated to the *Circulation of the Sermons Abroad*, while the topmost twigs, on which I can plainly read the words *Foreign Translations of Sermons*, bid fair to rival in all respects their older companions. To me, *their* rapid growth is most cheering, for their leaves contain so much of the essential oil of "the Tree of Life" that they are in a very literal sense "for the healing of the nations". One shoot of the lemon tree, which drooped awhile, but now flourishes as freely as the other branches, symbolizes the *Auxiliary Book Fund*; another reminds me of *The Sword and the Trowel distribution*, while the many thousands of *tracts and pamphlets* which are circulated by the Fund are well represented by the twigs and leaves which spring from the larger stems.'

All through, Mrs Spurgeon was herself a most generous donor to the Book Fund finances, her personal services being supplemented by monetary gifts far greater than is generally supposed; while by her will the Fund benefits to a considerable extent.

Chapter 13

LAST YEARS OF MARRIED LIFE

In 1880 Mr and Mrs Spurgeon removed from Nightingale Lane, Clapham, to 'Westwood', Beulah Hill, Norwood, their last home on earth. The remarkable circumstances attending the sale of the old house and the purchase of the new have been told fully in *The Life of Charles Haddon Spurgeon*, and it is unnecessary to repeat the story here. The new home was a great improvement on the old; not only was it situated farther from the smoke and noise of London, but the rooms were much more ample and convenient than those of Helensburgh House, and the grounds covered nearly nine acres. The actual changing, however, was a time of much discomfort, although Mrs Spurgeon's health was far better than it had been for a long time past.

'What a stirring up of one's quiet nest this removal is,' she wrote in her diary, 'and how tenderly one learns to look on familiar objects from which we are to be parted for ever. The heart yearns over a place endeared by an intimate acquaintance of twenty-three years and full of happy and solemn associations. Every nook and corner, both of house and garden, abounds with sweet or sorrowful memories, and the remembrance of manifold mercies cling like a rich tapestry to the walls of the desolate rooms. On this spot nearly a quarter of a century of blissful wedded life has been passed, and though both husband and wife have been called to suffer severe physical pain and months of weakness within its boundary, our house has been far oftener a "Bethel" to us than a "Bochim". The very walls might cry out against us as ungrateful did we not silence them by our ceaseless thanksgiving, for the Lord has here loaded us with benefits and consecrated every inch of space with tokens of his great lovingkindness. The sun of his goodness has photographed every portion of our dear home upon our hearts, and though other lights and shadows must be reflected there in coming days, they can never obliterate the sweet images which grateful memory will jealously preserve. Tender remembrance will render indelible the pictures of the sick chamber – which so many times had almost been "the gate of heaven" to our spirit; the little room, tenderly fitted up by a husband's careful love, and so often the scene of a scarcely-hoped-for convalescence; the study – sacred to the Pastor's earnest work and silent witness of wrestlings and communings known only to God and his own soul; the library – where the shelves gladly suffered a constant spoliation and renewal for the blessed work of the Book Fund.

'It is hard to leave all these sympathetic surroundings and dwell in the house of a stranger, but we believe we have seen the cloudy pillar move, and heard our Leader's voice bidding us "go forward", so in trustful obedience we strike our tent and prepare to depart to the "place of which he has told us". And our new home may be to us a "Tabor" if our Lord will but dwell with us there.'

After the removal, Mrs Spurgeon was delighted with her new home. 'In spite of the turmoil and trouble caused by the painful process of removal,' she writes, 'our first fortnight on Beulah's Hill has been a time of great and unaccustomed joy. Blest for this period with a singular accession of health and strength, the new owners together visited the various spots of interest in their little kingdom, making pleasant discoveries every day; now tracing a winding garden path to some unexpected opening, now looking with growing admiration upon the glorious views of earth and sky, ever breathing the bright, clear air with a lively sense of exhilaration and refreshment, and constantly pausing to marvel at the goodness of God in "choosing such an inheritance for them". It seems almost like living a new life, and as if pain and sickness were left behind in the valley for ever . . . These bright days and golden hours may not last long, but they are very precious in present possession, and will leave blissful memories behind them.'

On Saturdays, here, as in their other homes, husband and wife would work together in the preparation of the sermon which the former was to deliver on the coming morning, and happy indeed were the time thus spent. Sometimes when the preacher had been unable to settle upon a text, he would say, 'Wifey, what shall I do? God has not given me a text yet', and Mrs Spurgeon would comfort him as well as she could. Perhaps she would be able to suggest a suitable passage, in which case her husband, after preaching, would give her due credit in referring to the sermon by saying: 'You gave me that text.'

When the lady was called into the study on these Saturday evenings by her husband there was always an easy chair, she tells us, drawn up to the table by

Mr Spurgeon's side, and a number of open books piled one upon another from which she used to read as directed by her husband. 'With these old volumes around him he was like a honey-bee amid the flowers; he seemed to know how to extract and carry off the sweet spoils from the most unpromising-looking tome among them. His acquaintance with them was so familiar and complete that he could at once place his hand on any author who had written upon the portion of Scripture which was engaging his attention; and I was, in this pleasant fashion, introduced to many of the Puritan and other divines, whom otherwise I might not have known.'

The change to Norwood, it was anticipated, might be of benefit to C. H. Spurgeon's health, and render unnecessary those annual winterings at Menton. But this did not prove to be the case. His painful ailment continued, and the sad partings of husband and wife had to go on year after year, he thinking of her in the lonely house in England, she full of anxiety for the loved one away on the Riviera, whose agony from the gout was oftentimes beyond endurance.

But even then his letters to his wife were full of humour, so as to cheer her and make things seem as bright as possible. 'I feel as if I were emerging from a volcano', he once wrote at the commencement of a convalescence, and on the notepaper he had sketched a hill from the crater of which his head and shoulders were rising. As time went on the preacher's illnesses became longer, and the painfulness of his malady more acute. In November 1890, he went to Menton full of hope, and on arriving wrote to Mrs Spurgeon: 'What heavenly sunshine! This is like another world. I cannot quite believe myself to be on the same planet. God grant that this may set me all right! Only three other visitors in the hotel – three American ladies – room *for you*.'

But the next day the dreadful gout attacked the patient's right hand and arm. Even then he wrote: 'The day is like one in Eden before our first parents fell. When my head is better I shall enjoy it. I have *eau de Cologne* dripped on to my hot brain-box; and as I have nothing to do, but to look out on the perfect scene before me, my case is not a "bad one". The attack, however, increased in virulence, and for eight days he was unable himself to write to Mrs Spurgeon; but he sent a message through his private secretary: 'Give her my love, and say I am very bad, and I wish I were at home for her to nurse me; but as I am not, I shall be helped through somehow.' Then came a letter, almost unreadable, so difficult a task had the tracing of the characters been: 'Beloved, to lose right hand is to be dumb. I am better, except at night. Could not love his darling more. Wished myself at home when pains came, but when worst this soft clear air helps me. It is as heaven's gate. All is well. Thus have I stammered a line or two. Not quite dumb, bless the Lord! What a good Lord he is! I shall yet praise him. Sleeplessness cannot so embitter the night as to make me fear when he is near.' The letter was signed, 'Your own beloved *Benjamite*' – a humorous reference to the fact that it had been written with the left hand.

After this, progress was slow, but such expressions as, 'Oh, that you were here!' clearly show how he longed to have his wife by his side. On 8th December he wrote, gleefully: 'To-day I dressed myself', and concluded, 'You write so sweetly. Yours is a hand which sets to music all it writes to me. God bless you! But you don't say how you are. If you do not, I will write every day.' Mrs Spurgeon had lovingly sought to conceal her own weakness, so as not to give any additional pain to her husband. When the English winter proved to be very cold, he wrote: 'Poor darling to be so cold. The Lord will soon hear prayer and send the soft South wind upon you, and then I also shall get well, and go out for walks and praise his Name. I wish I could think of something to cast a gleam of sunlight over "Westwood". If my love were light you would live in the sun. I shall send you some roses, to-morrow, and they will prophesy of better days', and a few days later: 'I keep on praying for change of weather for you and the poor and sick. I wish I could send you a brazier of the coals of my heart, which have a most vehement flame.'

Such was the correspondence which passed between this devoted couple in the closing days of their united lives, for although Mrs Spurgeon's own letters are not available, it is clear from a reference here and there in her husband's replies that they were of a like loving character.

Christmas was passed by the preacher in much pain, which, however, did not prevent him 'digging away at books and letters'. Then on New Year's Day, 1891, he writes: 'A happy New Year to you, my sweetest and best! I would write it in the biggest of capitals if that would show how happy I wish this year to be . . . I have been for a drive in the delicious summer sunshine. Oh, that you had been at my side! I have just read your sweet, sweet letter. You best-beloved of my heart, how I wish I could change your weather! I can only pray; but prayer moves the hand which moves winds and clouds. The Lord himself comfort you and bear you up under all troubles, and make up to you, by his own presence, the absence of health, warmth and husband!' Then on Mrs Spurgeon's birthday she received a letter in which her husband said: 'I trust this will reach you on your own dear birthday. Ten thousand benedictions be upon you! What an immeasurable blessing you have been to me and are still. Your patience in suffering and diligence in service are works of the Holy Spirit in you for which I adore his Name. Your love to me is not only a product of nature, but it has been so sanctified by grace that it has become a spiritual blessing to me. May you still be upheld, and if you may not be kept from suffering, may you be preserved from sinking!'

All this time, although suffering so severely herself, Mrs Spurgeon was working indefatigably to help others. The Book Fund and the Pastors' Aid Fund were in full swing, and in order to give some relief to the poor of Thornton Heath, who were thrown out of work and in dire straits on account of the prolonged frost, she opened a soup kitchen at Westwood, and distributed coals freely among the people. C. H. Spurgeon hearing of this, wrote: 'I am so glad you feed the poor; spend £10 for me, please; don't stint anything.'

At last on 2nd February the patient, apparently much improved in health, started for England, writing to his wife on the same morning a note which concluded with the words, 'Blessed be God that we are spared to each other.' But the apparent improvement was far from being real or permanent.

This is not the place in which to give a detailed account of C. H. Spurgeon's final days in England. He preached at the Tabernacle for the last time on Sunday morning, 7th June 1891, and then directly afterwards his illness took an alarming turn, and a fatal issue was feared.

Mrs Spurgeon was an indefatigable nurse, and the sympathy of the whole nation went out to her in her sore trial. Mr Gladstone wrote: 'In my own home, darkened at the present time, I have read with sad interest the daily accounts of Mr Spurgeon's illness, and I cannot help conveying to you the earnest assurance of my sympathy with you and with him, and of my cordial admiration, not only of his splendid powers, but still more of his devoted and unfailing character. May I humbly commend you and him in all contingencies to the infinite stores of the divine love and mercy.' Many other distinguished people, including a number of the Bishops, also wrote to Mrs Spurgeon.

The patient did not get better, and on 26th October he started for Menton, accompanied this time by his wife, as well as by a number of friends. Later, Miss E. H. Thorne, Mrs Spurgeon's companion and friend, joined the party, and these two ladies took it in turns to nurse the invalid who at first seemed to benefit by the warm Southern sun.

But on 20th January serious symptoms set in and Mr Spurgeon had to take to his bed, from which he never again rose. After remaining unconscious for five days he passed away on 31st January 1892, in the presence of his wife and four intimate friends. The loss, as may be imagined, was a terrible one for the devoted wife, but she was sustained by the knowledge that sooner or later she would join her husband where there are no more partings. In the death chamber, so soon as the first shock was over, the little party knelt down, and Mr Harrald, the preacher's private secretary, offered prayer, being followed by Mrs Spurgeon, who thanked the Lord for the precious treasure so long lent to her, and sought at the throne of grace strength and guidance for the future.

Later she was able to cable to her son Thomas, in Australia, 'Father in heaven. Mother resigned.' From all parts of the world messages of condolence reached her, those from England including expressions of sympathy from our present King and Queen [Edward VII and Queen Alexandra]. The body was removed to this country for burial without delay, and Mrs Spurgeon sent with the remains a number of palm branches from Menton to be placed round the coffin while it stood in the Tabernacle.

Mrs Spurgeon herself remained on the Riviera for some time longer as the guest of Mr Hanbury at La Mortola. 'There amid the olive-groves and rose-covered terraces,' she says, 'the dear Master taught me *His* estimate of true affection by recalling to my mind his own words to his disciples, "If ye loved me, ye would rejoice, because I go to the Father", and thus he made me understand that the thought of my darling's everlasting bliss must overcome and banish my own selfish grief and sorrow.'

Chapter 14

WIDOWHOOD

Mrs Spurgeon's widowhood lasted close upon a dozen years, and in a sense, her life, since 1892, must have been a singularly lonely one, although she had her two sons always near to comfort and cheer her, and the many friends of her late husband were ever ready to meet any wish she might express. Grief, however, did not occupy her to the exclusion of useful and thoughtful work. In fact, her last years were, taking into consideration her growing age and infirmity, her busiest. The Book Fund was never allowed to flag; the Pastors' Aid Fund was ever ready to help deserving ministers in sore financial straits, and all the other branches of the original organization were kept in a flourishing condition.

Then Mrs Spurgeon gave a good deal of time to literary work, her *magnum opus* of course being *C. H. Spurgeon's Autobiography, compiled from his Diary, Letters and Records*, in which she had the assistance of Mr Harrald [Spurgeon's secretary, J. W. Harrald]. This, as is generally known, is a monumental work in four large volumes,[1] and it occupied Mrs Spurgeon several years in the preparation, all her husband's correspondence, sermons and books being carefully sifted in order to provide the material for the auto-biography. Mrs Spurgeon herself wrote the chapters dealing with the home and conjugal life of her husband, and these in many places show the pathetic longing she always had to join him. 'Ah! my husband,' she says in one passage, 'the blessed earthly ties which we welcomed so rapturously are dissolved now, and death has hidden thee from my mortal eyes; but not even death can divide thee from me or sever the love which united our hearts so closely. I feel it living and growing still, and I believe it will find its full and spiritual development only when we shall meet in the glory-land and worship together before the throne!'

This was written in 1898, and a comparison with a passage from her Book Fund report for 1891 will show how time and work had helped her to a holy resignation in waiting for the longed-for reunion. 'Oh! my husband, my husband,' she wrote in the

---

[1] A revised edition in two volumes was published by the Banner of Truth Trust in 1962 and 1973.

earlier year, 'every moment of my now desolate life I wonder how I can live without thee! The heart that for so many years has been filled and satisfied with thy love must needs be very empty and stricken now that thou art gone!'

As a writer, Mrs Spurgeon had a rare literary gift, and her style was not unlike that of her husband. It was at C. H. Spurgeon's suggestion that she undertook, while yet Miss Susannah Thompson, to assist him in compiling a little book of extracts from the writings of the Puritan divine, Thomas Brooks. Her lover had asked her to go through 'an ancient, rusty-looking book', marking all the paragraphs and sentences that seemed particularly sweet, quaint or instructive, and with much fear and trembling the young girl complied. The result was a small volume entitled *Smooth Stones Taken from Ancient Brooks*, and this book, Mrs Spurgeon's first literary effort, has just been reprinted [1903] by Messrs. Passmore and Alabaster.

Ten Years of My Life in the Service of the Book Fund, and *Ten Years After*, have already been referred to, but perhaps the best of Mrs Spurgeon's literary work will be found in three dainty little devotional volumes entitled, respectively, *A Carillon of Bells to Ring out the Old Truths of Free Grace and Dying Love*;

A Cluster of Camphire, or, Words of Cheer and Comfort for Sick and Sorrowful Souls; and, *A Basket of Summer Fruit*. Each volume is perfect in its way. In *A Carillon of Bells*, for instance, one can hear the very bells ringing on every page, and in the whole range of devotional literature it would be difficult to find anything sweeter or having a truer ring than the opening words on the text, 'He that spared not his own Son . . . how shall he not with him also freely give us all things':

'Dear Lord, faith's fingers are joyfully touching the keys of this carillon of sweet bells this morning, and making them ring jubilantly to the praise of your Name!

> *How shall he not!*
> *How shall he not!*
> *He that spared not!*
> *How shall he not!*

What a peal of absolute triumph it is! Not a note of doubt or uncertainty mars the heavenly music. Awake, my heart, and realize that is *your faith* which is making such glorious melody! You can scarcely believe it for gladness? Yet it is happily true, for the Lord himself has given the grace, and then accepts the tribute of gratitude and praise which that grace brings. Press the tuneful keys again, for faith holds festival today, and the joy of assurance is working wonders.

He that spared not!
How shall he not!

Hear how the repeated negatives gloriously affirm the fact of his readiness to bless! These silver bells have truly the power to drive away all evil things.'

In addition to these volumes, Mrs Spurgeon is the author of a number of 'Westwood Leaflets' on devotional and other topics, and was for years a very frequent contributor to *The Sword and the Trowel,* for the conduct of which until recently she was responsible. Another work in which she took a great and prayerful interest was the selection of the daily texts for *Spurgeon's Illustrated Almanac,* and the preparation of that little booklet for publication. For about thirty years she chose the passages of Scripture, and this was no light work, when year after year fresh texts had to be found, which would fulfil the two necessary conditions of being short and also helpful when taken apart from their contexts.

Other kinds of work, too, Mrs Spurgeon did, and did with all her accustomed zeal. In 1895, for instance, when 'Westwood' was being redecorated, she went to Bexhill to stay for a time, and learning that the town possessed no Baptist Chapel, she began to pray and work for the establishment of one. As the result of her efforts a school-chapel was first opened, and in 1897 Mrs Spurgeon herself laid the foundation-stone of a fine sanctuary, 'To the glory of God, and in perpetual remembrance of her beloved husband's blameless life, forty years' public ministry and still continued proclamation of the gospel by his printed sermons.' This chapel was opened free of debt in the following year. In 1899 again, during the collecting of subscriptions for the erection of the present Metropolitan Tabernacle, which was to take the place of the first building, Mrs Spurgeon not only generously contributed to the Rebuilding Fund, but on a certain day – 8th February – she held a reception in the basement of the Tabernacle, and at one sitting received from those who attended about £6,367 towards the Fund.

In the summer of 1903 Mrs Spurgeon had a severe attack of pneumonia which prostrated her, and from this she never recovered, being confined to her bed. One or other of her sons visited their mother almost daily to comfort and cheer her in the closing days of her life. Gradually she sank, and in the first week of September the flame of life seemed so feeble that it was expected to flicker out. Even then Mrs Spurgeon manifested her strong faith in the God whom she had trusted for so long. 'Though he slay me, yet will I trust in him', she said feebly, and quoted the lines:

> His love in times past forbids me to think
> He'll leave me at last in trouble to sink,

asking those in the room to complete the verse.

But there was a tenacity of life about this weak woman which was little expected. Week after week she lingered, though getting weaker as each day passed. On 7th October she gave her parting blessing to her son Thomas. 'The blessing, the double blessing, of your father's God be upon you and upon your brother', she said, and then a few moments later, 'Good-bye, Tom; the Lord bless you for ever and ever! Amen.' When very near the end she clasped her feeble hands together, and, her face aglow with a heavenly radiance, exclaimed: 'Blessed Jesus! Blessed Jesus! I can see the King in his glory!'

Mrs Spurgeon passed away peacefully at half-past eight on the morning of Thursday, 22nd October 1903. She was buried at Norwood Cemetery in the grave where her husband's remains lay, and Pastor

Archibald Brown, who spoke such beautiful words at the interment of C. H. Spurgeon, joined with Pastor Sawday in conducting the funeral service over the remains of the great preacher's wife.

Chapter 15

CONCLUSION

Mrs Spurgeon has gone, but her work remains. Her last thoughts were for the Book Fund, and for the poor ministers who are benefited by its aid; and by her will she left a sum of money for the assistance of the work which owed its inception and its continued success to her untiring zeal. Further, she had expressed a wish that her friend and companion of forty years, Miss E. H. Thorne, should carry on the Book Fund with its various branches, in conjunction with Pastor J. S. Hockey.

Miss Thorne has willingly agreed to do this, and her enthusiasm for the work being second only to Mrs Spurgeon's, it will be a matter for satisfaction to all Christian people who followed with interest the efforts of the deceased lady, that there will be no cessation in the conduct of the Book Fund. C. H. Spurgeon once wrote: 'This good work of providing mental food for ministers ought never to cease till their incomes are doubled. May "Mrs Spurgeon's Book Fund" become a permanent source of blessing to ministers and churches!'

The work must not flag for lack of funds, and as the demand has always been so much greater than the supply, the wherewithal to provide the books cannot be received too quickly. That the devoted woman who originated the Fund, who conducted it with such splendid success for so long, and who gave so generously in her lifetime of her services and substance, has left some money for the Fund will doubtless only act as an incentive to other 'stewards of the Lord' to give liberally, so that this important effort may more and more cope with the need which led to its institution. As a tribute to the memory of Mrs Spurgeon, what could be better than a gift to the Book Fund which will still bear her name?

If greatness depends upon the amount of good which one does in the world, if it is only another name for unselfish devotion in the service of others – and surely true greatness is all this – then Mrs C. H. Spurgeon will go down to posterity as one of the greatest women of her time.